95⁰
3245E

This belongs to
Charles Fitzgerald

D0194036

Splendor
of the Gods

The Grand Tour

Splendor of the Gods

Flavio Conti

Translated by Patrick Creagh

HBJ Press
a subsidiary of Harcourt Brace Jovanovich, Inc.
Boston

HBJ Press

President, Robert J. George

Publisher, Giles Kemp

Vice President, Richard S. Perkins, Jr.

Managing Director, Valerie S. Hopkins

Executive Editor, Marcia Heath

Series Editor, Carolyn Hall

Staff Editor, Chris Heath

Text Editors: Amanda Heller, William McBee

Editorial Production: Karen E. English, Ann
   McGrath, Eric Brus, Betsie Brownell,
   Patricia Leal, Pamela George

Project Coordinator, Linda S. Behrens

Business Manager, Edward Koman

Marketing Director, John R. Whitman

Public Relations, Janet Schotta

Business Staff: Pamela Herlich, Joan Kenney

Architectural Consultant, Dennis J. DeWitt

Text Consultants: Janet Adams, Elizabeth R.
   DeWitt, Perween Hasan

Design Implementation, Designworks

Rizzoli Editore

Authors of the Italian Edition: Jiri Burian,
   Dr. Flavio Conti, Henri Stierlin, Jersy
   Szablowski, Dr. Gian Maria Tabarelli

Idea and Realization, Harry C. Lindinger

General Supervisor, Luigi U. Re

Graphic Designer, Gerry Valsecchi

Coordinator, Vilma Maggioni

Editorial Supervisor, Gianfranco Malafarina

Research Organizer, Germano Facetti

U.S. Edition Coordinator, Natalie Danesi
   Murray

Photography Credits

Aerofilms: pp. 74–75/ *Almasy:* p. 156 top/ *Cauchetier:* pp. 138–143, p. 144 top, p. 144 bottom left, pp. 145–148/ *Fabbrica del Duomo:* p. 18, pp. 20–32/ *W. Forman:* p. 109, p. 111 top left/ *Foto 2000:* p. 12 left/ *Hassia:* p. 83, p. 85, p. 87 bottom/ *Hassmann:* p. 57, pp. 58–60, p. 61 top, pp. 62–68/ *Hornak:* p. 80, p. 82, p. 86, p. 88 bottom, pp. 91–92, pp. 94–95/ *Internationales Bildarchio:* p. 157/ *Kodansha:* pp. 105–107, p. 110, p. 111 bottom, pp. 112–115/ *Magnum Berry:* p. 76 bottom, p. 77/ *Magnum Burri:* pp. 153–155, p. 156 bottom, pp. 158–164/ *Magnum G. Rodger:* p. 79 bottom, p. 96/ *Marka-Orion Press:* p. 108 bottom/ *Photri:* p. 108 top/ *Publiaerphoto:* pp. 10–11/ *Radici:* p. 61 bottom/ *Rizzoli:* p. 76 top/ *Scala:* p. 9, p. 12 right, pp. 13–17, p. 19/ *Sheridan:* p. 73, p. 78, p. 79 top, p. 81, p. 84, p. 87 top left and right, p. 88 top, pp. 89–90, p. 93, p. 137, p. 144 bottom right, p. 146 top left/ *Shogakukan-Zido:* p. 116/ *Stierlin:* pp. 41–52, pp. 121–132.

© 1977 by Rizzoli Editore-International Division
Copyright © 1978 by HBJ Press, Inc.

All rights reserved. No part of this publication may be reproduced or transmitted in any form or by any means, electronic or mechanical, including photocopy, recording, or any information storage and retrieval system, without permission in writing from the publisher.

Library of Congress Catalog Card Number: 78–51424
ISBN: 0-15-003727-9

Printed in Hong Kong by Mandarin Publishers Ltd.

Contents

Preface
Splendor of the Gods

Non nobis, sed tibi, Domine ("Not for us, but for Thee, O God"). This was the sentiment that inspired the massive European cathedrals of the Middle Ages. The faithful spared neither physical effort nor personal sacrifice to show their adoration of the Lord and to prepare a testimony to their belief. With willing hands and generous hearts they contributed their skills, labor, and money to serve God and to express His glory in stone.

But building exalted religious edifices is not peculiar to Christianity. All over the world, men of all religions have expressed their faith by the construction of towering temples for their gods. The same spirit that induced Solomon to build the Temple of Jerusalem inspired the Incas and Hindus, Buddhists and Moslems, to glorify their deities by giving the best of themselves. Throughout history, the divinity has always deserved the fattest calf and the richest cloth—and the most magnificent place of worship.

However, if faith is the same the world over, the architectural forms it inspires are almost infinite in their variety. Take, for instance, the Duomo of Milan. This cathedral is especially dear to the Milanese just because it is like no other in the world—although throughout the centuries, it was often reviled by the very citizens who were paying for it. The cathedral's singularity was largely determined by the long and complex history of its construc-tion. Some four hundred years after the first stone was laid, Napoleon Bonaparte finally brought the work to completion, and in 1805, he had himself crowned king of Italy within its walls.

The Duomo was built in its own version of the Gothic—a style little favored elsewhere in Italy. With its immense triangular façade and riot of confectionery decoration—turrets, spires, buttresses, and more than three thousand statues—it is an impressive and unmistakable landmark in the center of Milan.

Just as the Duomo was built in a style which was essentially "foreign" to the Italian eye, other buildings in this volume also illustrate the adaptation of an "alien" style. The temple complex at Horyuji, near Nara, is an example. Constructed in the early years of the seventh century, these buildings are among the first Buddhist temples in Japan and reveal elements of their Chinese and Korean precursors in both architecture and ornamentation. However, the foreign and indigenous elements of the design merge to produce a harmonious style which now appears absolutely characteristic of Japan. Elegant and graceful, the temple complex at Horyuji, arranged in an innovative asymmetric plan, is also famous as the oldest group of wooden buildings in the world.

The Cathedral of Mexico City is another example of a synthesis of "foreign" and "indigenous" architecture. When the Spanish conquistadors arrived in Mexico, they introduced Catholicism and erected cathedrals and churches modeled after those at home. However, the colorful Indian influence remained strong in Mexico, enriching the restrained architecture of Spain to form a variant of the style that was distinctly Mexican.

Building began on the Cathedral of Mexico City in 1573, some fifty years after Cortes first arrived at the court of the Aztec ruler Montezuma. The church, designed by Spanish architects, is based on the plan of the Cathedral of Salamanca in Spain. But it was built by Indian artisans and constructed on the foundations of Aztec pyramids that had once stood on the site.

Many hundreds of years before the Cathedral of Mexico City was built, a Saxon king constructed another monument to the Christian faith on a small island in the Thames known as Thorney Island. Some four hundred years later, this spot was to be rededicated as Westminster Abbey—the abbey which the pious King Edward the Confessor made the heart of his kingdom. Since that time, it has remained linked with the destiny of England and has become its beloved national shrine and monument.

During its rich history, Westminster Abbey has not only served as a church and monastery but has also fulfilled many secular functions. It has been at different times a parliament, a mausoleum, and even a repository for the standards for the Royal Mint. Today, it also contains a museum in the Norman undercroft, or crypt.

The Cathedral of St. Stephen in Vienna is also a religious shrine as well as a national monument. Originally a Romanesque parish church in the city, it later became the seat of the Holy Roman Empire and stood as a symbolic affirmation of Christianity for the Viennese in their struggles against domination by the Moslem Turks. St. Stephen's has always been at the heart of Viennese life. Its precincts are a meeting place for the inhabitants of the city, and in the days before newspapers, proclamations of popes and emperors were posted on its massive door. Even today, on New Year's Eve, radios all over Austria tune to Vienna to hear the great bell Pummering toll the changing year. Standing in the center of Vienna, the cathedral dominates the city, looking far out over the Vienna Woods beyond.

Like St. Stephen's, the Mosque of the Shah in Isfahan in central Iran dominates its surroundings. The mosque is named after its creator, Shah Abbas I, who made Isfahan the seat of his kingdom. The shah undertook elaborate and splendid construction in his new capital, building palaces, bridges, gardens, and the beautiful Royal Square. On this square stands the magnificent mosque, which is both a dwelling of Allah and a tribute to the temporal power of the shah. The shah's mosque is also called the Blue Mosque because of its deep-blue decorative tiles and great blue-green dome. With graceful arcades and slim minarets and the serene water-filled courtyard, the mosque attests to the splendor of Moslem architecture.

To those unversed in Hindu philosophy, the Kandarya Mahadeva—greatest of the thirty-five sanctuaries at Khajuraho in the middle of northern India—seems more like a secular than a religious building. Erotic sculptures decorate the friezes of the temple, and within the *garbha-griha,* or inner sanctum, stands the *lingam,* or phallic symbol of the divine power. This temple is a center of the Hindu cult of Shiva, the god of destruction and regeneration. Khajuraho was the capital of the Candella dynasty, and its temples were consequently more accessible than other similar "erotic" shrines, which were usually built in remote places to avoid shocking or exciting non-initiates.

The Kandarya Mahadeva and Chartres Cathedral evolved from vastly different architectural traditions. Set among the wheat fields of northern France, the town of Chartres boasts a Gothic cathedral renowned above all others for its structural purity and the beauty of its ornamentation. Built in only twenty-seven years, the cathedral is lavishly embellished with sculptures which retell familiar Bible stories—the coming of Christ, the Last Judgment, the Annunciation—as do its legendary stained-glass windows (nearly all of which are original). The windows also depict scenes from the daily lives of the people, whose taxes and hard labor built the cathedral, and show the peasants themselves as witnesses to the Passion and other Biblical scenes. The soaring steeple and bell tower and the famous flying buttresses seem to reach toward Heaven, expressing the yearning of the congregation for spiritual peace. The Cathedral of Chartres, perhaps more than any of the other buildings in this volume, seems to have been created by the faith of men, paid for by their sacrifices, and adorned through their hope of salvation. It is a wonderfully human house of God.

All of these eight buildings are both godly dwellings and reflections of the nations and individuals who built them. Perhaps this is the greatest inherent contradiction of religious architecture: The largest, most complex tributes to a divinity inspire awe precisely because of the human accomplishments they represent. *Non nobis, sed tibi, Domine.* But despite this dedication to the deity, it was human aspiration and faith, along with human ability and energy, which built these remarkable religious monuments.

Duomo of Milan

Italy

Preceding page, the Duomo and the Piazza del Duomo. The domed building giving onto the piazza is Milan's famous Galleria. The open space of the piazza emphasizes the monumental scale of the cathedral. For centuries—until the advent of the skyscraper—a tacit agreement forbade other buildings to overshadow the lofty Duomo.

The exterior of the Duomo is encrusted with a series of vertical architectural features—pillars, buttresses, spires, statues, and reliefs—which give the building a rich voluptuousness (right). Details of the façade (far right, above and below) depict a few of the statues that decorate the Duomo. There are also innumerable reliefs and other decorative stone carvings. Five bronze doors (detail below)—all twentieth-century work—open onto the nave and aisles.

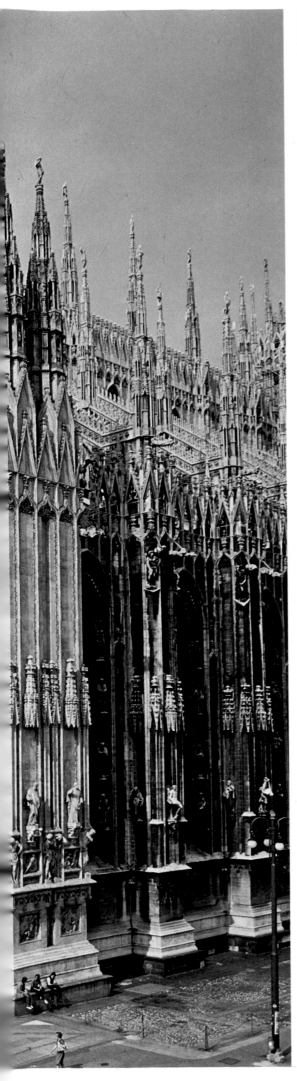

The façade of the Duomo is lavishly adorned with exuberant seventeenth- and eighteenth-century detail applied to a medieval shell. The elaborate ornamentation of the cathedral has been compared to the work of a whimsical confectioner. The cupola is almost hidden behind its stone tracery. Its filigreed spire and gilt statue of the Virgin, to whom the cathedral is dedicated, rise high above the lacy walls of the church (above).

Left, a few of the 169 windows that lighten the façade and balance the mass of detail. They also unite the solid base of the building with its airy upper levels.

The play of the flying buttresses on the side walls and the exterior of the apse (facing page) is typically Gothic, although their use at the Duomo—solely as supports for the gutters that carry off rainwater—is not. The detailed decoration on the outside of the cathedral is continually threatened by smog and corroding acids in the city air. Its preservation is now the charge of the Fabbrica del Duomo, the body originally responsible for building the cathedral.

The cathedral's spires and pinnacles, surmounted by statues (right), have dominated the skyline of Milan for centuries. The oldest statue dates from the fifteenth century. It was commissioned by Marco Carelli, a wealthy citizen who spent a large sum to have the figure of Saint George by Giorgio Solari erected on the only spire then in existence. According to tradition, the features are those of Gian Galeazzo Visconti. Far right, a statue attired as a Roman soldier. The statue dearest to the hearts of the Milanese, and the symbol of the city, is the Madonnina, which is set on top of the central spire (above and detail far right). The statue, which rises 350 feet above the city, is made of gilded bronze and dates from 1774.

Nearly every major sculptor of northern Italy from the fifteenth century to the present has worked on the Duomo, so that the cathedral is, in a sense, an open-air museum of Lombard sculpture. Particularly strange and fascinating are the gargoyles that serve, as they do in other Gothic cathedrals, to carry off rainwater. The diverse subjects chosen for these extraordinary drainpipes include grotesque dragons, sea horses, mastiffs, fish, and reptiles. Sometimes they are supported by giants (below), either nude or exotically clothed as great lords in fancy vestments, knights in armor, or even pilgrims.

While the gargoyles are generally the work of lesser artists or apprentices whose names are unknown, the Duomo's thousands of statues and reliefs are often signed. Some are by famous artists, including Jacopino de Tradate, Matteo Raverti, Andrea Fusina, Ludovico Pogliaghi, and members of the Solari and Amadeo families. There are more than 3,000 statues in all, of which about 1,800 are on the roof. Many of the statues on the spires, however, are modern copies whose originals are kept in the Duomo Museum to protect them from smog. Even now, new statues are being commissioned to fill places that have been empty for centuries.

Above and above right, statues of Eve and Adam by Christoforo Solari.

Right, the sons of Noah.

The tiburium, which is the exterior structure of the cupola (detail above), and the flying buttresses (left) were the parts of the Duomo most severely criticized by the foreign builders and architects who were called in to direct the work. These outsiders were always dismissed, often after an extremely short stay, because of their inability to adapt to the techniques of the local laborers. Many of these architects predicted the total collapse of the structure, and each recommended a different solution. Throughout the fifteenth century, one project after another for the tiburium was turned down. Finally, in 1490, a design submitted by Amadeo and Dolcebuono, based on an octagonal structure, was accepted. The basic structure of the tiburium was then built in less than ten years. Despite all the dire predictions, the cathedral has withstood time, earthquakes, and bombardment.

Facing page, grotesque gargoyles at the ends of flying buttresses along the south side of the nave.

The roof of the Duomo, contrary to Gothic tradition, has a modest incline. The roof is composed of a series of gently sloping terraces originally covered with tiles, which were replaced in the nineteenth century with large sheets of marble. Flights of dizzying steps—some in the wall itself and some climbing up between the spires, the balustrades, and the flying buttresses—lead from one level to another. Early in this century, the Milanese who remained in town during August would gather to enjoy a little cool air on this vast terrace.

Facing page, the central nave which rises to a height of about 150 feet. Its ribbed vaults are borne on massive columns. This central nave is flanked by two aisles on each side, with an overall width of about 190 feet. The whole church is unusually large. Its exterior measures about 500 feet in length and 300 feet across at the transept. The transepts are flanked by side aisles. There are several altars along the sides and around the polygonal apse at the east end of the cathedral.

In the mighty rhythm of the pillars, the geometry of the cross vaults, and the dim light from the stained glass, the Duomo displays the mystical and awe-inspiring qualities common to all Gothic cathedrals (right). Several elements in the design of the cathedral, however, are peculiar to the Duomo, among them the unusual capitals of the huge columns, decorated with statues of saints, angels, and historical figures (below right). These statues introduced the faithful to central figures in Christian history. Their education was also furthered, both in the Duomo and in French cathedrals, by the stories depicted in the stained-glass windows and, in many Italian Gothic or Renaissance churches, by the great cycles of frescoes.

The interior decoration of the Duomo tells the story of the artisans and the varying architectural styles that contributed to the construction of the cathedral over the centuries. The altar of the Madonna of the Tree (above right) is the work of T. Rinaldi, L. M. Richini, and F. Mangone, all artists of the seventeenth century. The altar is named for the huge medieval candlestick, possibly of French origin, which stands in front of it (above left and detail left). As a whole and in its details, such as the figures of angels that surround the Madonna, the altar expresses the ability of Baroque artists to adapt successfully to the Gothic tone of the cathedral.

Facing page, one of the stained-glass windows of the Duomo. The windows of Gothic cathedrals explained the Bible and the mysteries of the faith to the largely illiterate congregations of the Middle Ages. Unfortunately, almost all the windows of the Duomo are reconstructions. Most of the originals were blown out by French artillery fire in 1796 during Napoleon's Italian campaign.

Above, an altar in the south transept, dedicated to Saint Giovanni Bono, who was Bishop of Milan in the eighth century.

The organs and organ lofts (above center) are incorporated into the very structure of the cathedral. They have two fronts, one facing the choir and the other the ambulatory. The original organs dated from the sixteenth century, but just before World War II, a new organ was completed. Much larger than the original, the organ consisted of seven different organs with a total of 15,200 pipes placed throughout the choir. The two pulpits, in gilded bronze and copper, were commissioned by Saint Carlo Borromeo and finished under his cousin, Cardinal Frederigo Borromeo.

Left, the effigy from the tomb of the Archbishop Ariberto da Intimiano, who died in 1040. According to tradition, he was the inventor of the Caroccio, the cart on which the Holy Sacrament and the banner of the city were carried into battle by the Milanese. Over the tomb is a large, copper crucifix (right) on which the figure of Christ is surrounded by a selection of symbols and figures: the sun, the moon, the Blessed Virgin, Saint John, and Ariberto himself.

Far right, a panel from the altar of Saint Ambrose, patron saint of Milan. It shows the birth of the saint, who is represented with a miraculous swarm of bees flying out of his mouth.

Above right, a bas-relief of the Virgin Mary with Saint Catherine and Saint Paul. The relief, the work of Jacomolo di Antonio, hangs over an altar designed by Pellegrini.

Left, a carved panel showing the Flight into Egypt.

Center, left, the Gothic altar of Saint Catherine, the only wooden altar that has remained to bear witness to the earliest days of the Duomo. Some scholars attribute it to the school of Campione. The gilt figure of the saint is a Baroque addition. Center, right, a painting of the Umbrian school, probably dating from 1394. It shows the Madonna of the Rose, named for the flower she holds in her left hand.

Below left, the sarcophagus by Jacopino de Tradate of Marco Carelli, an early benefactor of the church. Below the recumbent image are niches containing statues of the Evangelists as well as of the doctors of the Church.

Under the floor of the Duomo are the winter chapter house and the Chapel of St. Carlo Borromeo. The chapter house is a traditional meeting place for the members of the chapter of the cathedral in the winter, when the choir is too cold. Here, those who are confirmed as adults receive the sacrament. The vaults (above right) are the work of Pellegrini. The altar (below right) is surrounded by a ring of marble columns and an unusual balustrade. The remains of Saint Carlo Borromeo, Bishop of Milan from 1565 to 1584, are in a silver coffin that rests in the adjacent chapel.

Following page, the awesome triangular façade of the Duomo, seen from the piazza. Though construction of the cathedral began in 1386, the height of the nave and aisles, and, therefore, the general shape of the façade, was not determined for several years, until the plan of the mathematician Gabriele Stornaloco was accepted by the Fabbrica. Work was begun on the façade in the sixteenth century and was completed in the nineteenth century. The five bronze doors are twentieth-century additions.

Duomo of Milan Italy

For centuries, Milan Cathedral—il Duomo di Milano—has outraged architectural purists, delighted visitors, and been a source of pride to the people of the city. Its great triangular façade is a riot of confectionery decoration, encrusted with turrets, columns, carvings, and statues, all competing for attention. The enormous cathedral with its wide piazza is the centerpiece of Milan, dominating this thriving commercial city.

The history of the Duomo is as complex and involved as its appearance—at various times it has been called an exception, a miracle, an anthology, a contradiction, and a confirmation.

The Duomo is an exception because it is the only cathedral in Italy constructed predominantly in the late Northern European Gothic style.

It is a miracle because disputes between local craftsmen and the foreign masters so often halted construction that it is a wonder that the cathedral was ever actually finished. Though building began in 1386, the Duomo was not completed until the reign of Napoleon. Indeed, the work was not absolutely finished until this century, when the five bronze doors of the façade were put in place.

It is an anthology because, for four and a half centuries, every Italian artist of any repute was involved with, or at least consulted about, the project. So many master masons and engineers from France and Germany worked on the Duomo that the records of accounts kept in the archives are a virtual directory of the architects and builders in Europe.

Left, a ninth-century representation of the Basilica Jemale, which was later rededicated and renamed Santa Maria Maggiore.

Far left, a map of Milan at the beginning of the twelfth century, showing the main churches of the city before the destruction wrought in 1162 by Frederick I.

Left, a representation of an ancient seal showing the façade of Santa Maria Maggiore, the ninth-century church that occupied the site where the Duomo now stands.

Above, Gian Galeazzo Visconti (1351–1402), the first duke of Milan, holding a model of the Duomo.

Below, ground plan and cross section (right) of the Duomo in two drawings by C. Cesariani (1521). The nave is flanked by two aisles on each side, the transept is divided into a central nave with two flanking aisles, and at the east end, an ambulatory passes around a polygonal apse. The cathedral is about 500 feet long and 300 feet wide at the transept, while the peak of the central nave is 350 feet in height.

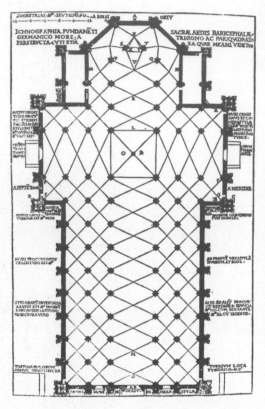

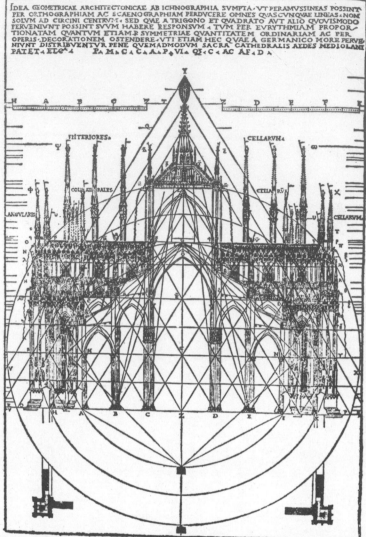

Below, a design for the cupola by Leonardo da Vinci. He submitted several plans, none of which was accepted.

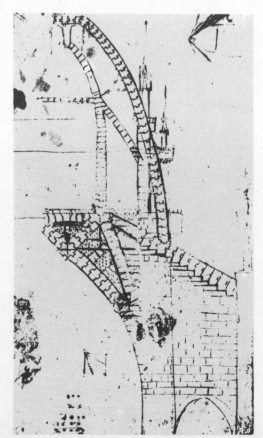

The Duomo is a contradiction because it is a cathedral in southern Europe that is in the late Gothic style of France and the Rhineland. Moreover, this resolutely Gothic cathedral was built over the course of centuries that saw the flowering and decline of the Renaissance, Baroque, and Neoclassical styles of architecture. Its design and its extravagant detail were created by hundreds of artisans loyal to various styles of building and decoration. As a result, the logic of the underlying conception seems eternally at war with much of the sculpture and many of the embellishments.

Finally, it is a confirmation in the sense that it supports the theory of Eugène Viollet-le-Duc. This nineteenth-century architect and writer stated that the Gothic cathedral, in addition to being a symbol of common piety, is a symbol of secular power striving against that of the Church. Like many other medieval cathedrals, the

Duomo was born out of an alliance between the city's powerful ruler and its religious hierarchy.

In the late fourteenth century, so the story goes, a strange malady afflicted the women of Milan—they were unable to bear healthy male children. Even Isabella of France, wife of Gian Galeazzo Visconti, Duke of Vertus and the ambitious ruler of Milan, had not been spared. Isabella had borne her husband three sons, and they had all died in infancy. The Duomo was planned by Gian Galeazzo as an offering to the Virgin Mary, both on his own account, as he wanted an heir, and on behalf of the people of Milan, who feared that their prosperous society might die out.

Gian Galeazzo decided to erect his new cathedral on the site of the ancient Basilica Jemale. The basilica, which had been rededicated to Mary and renamed Santa Maria Maggiore, had been the main

church of Milan since the time of Saint Ambrose, the patron saint of the city. The Church did not oppose this decision to demolish Milan's most sacred monument, for the archbishop was a close relative of the duke. By 1386, construction was ready to begin.

At this time, the late Gothic style was flourishing in the countries north of Italy. Gian Galeazzo wanted to become king of Italy, and he intended to build a church befitting a sovereign. To his mind, only the Gothic style of the magnificent cathedrals of France and Germany would serve such an exalted purpose. In addition, Milan had close relations with the various courts of France and Germany, and it was easy for Gian Galeazzo to turn to those countries for models and assistance. The duke himself was closely connected to France. His title derived from a French fief, the county of Vertus—although, with intentional irony, his Milanese subjects had

Italianized and corrupted his title to the "Duke of Virtu."

There was an Italian Gothic style that used the pointed arch and ribbed vault. With its large, smooth surfaces of multicolored marble, broad naves, and moderate play of light and shade, it was in other respects more severe and angular than late Gothic. The Italian taste for Classical proportions rejected excessive stress on the vertical in favor of a greater balance between height and width. In addition, the customary building material in Italy was brick rather than the stone used elsewhere in European Gothic cathedrals. Gian Galeazzo's decision to build in the northern style, therefore, was a deliberate rejection of Italian tradition and remained a source of aggravation among the builders of the Duomo—both local and foreign—for centuries to come.

A special body—the Fabbrica del Duomo—was established to arrange and

In the sixteenth and seventeenth centuries, the Duomo and its piazza were the center of life in the city.

Above left, an illustration of the festivities in celebration of the birth of the son of Philip IV of Spain in 1630. This print shows the façade of the earlier church.

Top, a seventeenth-century illustration of the funeral of Bishop Cesare Monti.

Above, the Duomo as it appeared in the first half of the eighteenth century, when Milan and the surrounding area were under Austrian rule.

oversee the project. The merchants and even the common people of Milan were generous in contributing toward the construction of the cathedral. No doubt fear of their powerful ruler encouraged some of the merchants to loosen their purse strings. But Milan was even then a commercial center of considerable impor-

Left, a seventeenth-century representation of the Duomo, complete with a hypothetical Baroque façade, showing Milan's two patron saints, Ambrose and Carlo Borromeo, looking down on the city.

Below left, another seventeenth-century representation of the cathedral, presumably a proposal for the design of the façade.

Below, a design for the façade of the Duomo by Carlo Buzzi, dating from the first half of the sixteenth century.

tance, and many merchants were trading with the countries of northern Europe. Their foreign travels encouraged admiration, even envy, for the grand northern cathedrals. Therefore, they readily supported the projected cathedral for their own city and ungrudgingly financed its construction: In fact, the budget of the Fabbrica was so sound that the funds for the Duomo were used to supplement the state treasury in hard times.

A Parade of Architects

The original architect of the Duomo is unknown, but it seems likely that he was a Frenchman. Executing the plans, however, soon became the task of Italians. In 1387, Simone da Orsenigo was appointed

Below, a design for a façade by the architects Hartel and Neckelman of Leipzig. Their design reached the final stage of a competition, sponsored by the Fabbrica from 1883 to 1886, seeking a design to replace the façade completed in 1813.

capomaestro, or principal architect.

By 1389, Gian Galeazzo had begun to fear that the ambitious project was too much for the local artisans. He called in a Frenchman, Nicholas de Bonaventure, to redesign the church. This appointment precipitated a rash of disputes. Within a year, the Frenchman was replaced by Johann von Freiburg from Germany who recommended that the height of the proposed building be considerably reduced. Von Freiburg, in his turn, was soon replaced by the Italian painter Giovannino De'Grassi.

By this time, the foundations had been laid and the walls and piers were being erected. But even at this stage, the Fabbrica began to question the proposed height of the building as well as the design of the columns, windows, and doors. They hired the mathematician Gabriele Stornaloco of Piacenza to provide yet another plan. His recommendation—that the façade be based upon an equilateral triangle—was eventually accepted and executed. Meanwhile, the Fabbrica engaged the German Heinrich Parler of Gmünd who, predictably enough, drew up a list of defects in the new design. His criticism was not well received by the Fabbrica. After a mere two months, Parler was dismissed for malfeasance and construction was halted. The year was 1392.

In those first six years, there had been a dizzying succession of builders and experts but no formal leader to shape and direct the project. As time went on, the post of chief architect became increasingly political. The foreign advisers invariably criticized the work of the Italian builders, who would then defend themselves vigorously and have the foreigners summarily dismissed.

The French and Germans had no respect for the instinctive building practices of the Italians, and the Italians had no use for the principles of late Gothic architecture. To the dismay of the foreign experts, the Italians covered the nave with an almost flat roof of half-cylindrical tiles rather than a high lead or slate roof supported on timber truss work. They used iron tie rods rather than other vaults or buttresses to oppose the thrusts of the vaults, and they employed flying buttresses simply to carry off water from the gutters.

After Heinrich Parler departed, Giovannino De'Grassi and Giacomo da Campione were left in possession of the field. This comparatively peaceful interlude lasted only eight years. Giovannino De'Grassi designed the tabernacle-shaped capitals of the columns but died in 1398. And only a few days later, his colleague followed him to the grave.

Further Disputes and Contradictions

By 1400, the parade of foreign and Italian architects was once again underway, and rivalries and accusations started up immediately. The Frenchman Jean Mignot prepared a lengthy statement declaring the building unsafe. He predicted that the whole edifice would soon collapse unless radical alterations were authorized. The outraged Italian craftsmen bridled at Mignot's suggested revisions and violently attacked his own design. Gian Galeazzo hired yet another German master to arbitrate in the dispute.

In 1402, work once again ground to a halt when Gian Galeazzo, in exasperation, deprived the Duomo of his financial support. He died not long afterward. The cathedral in which he had once hoped to be crowned king of Italy was still unfinished. After the death of the duke, the project lost impetus. Construction continued under the direction of a series of Italians, but none of them provided the artistic genius and guidance necessary for the project.

Pope Martin V consecrated the cathedral in 1418. The apse had been completed, and foundations had been laid for the columns of the nave and the side walls—but that was all. A temporary roof was erected to keep out the chill autumn winds. Still, the Duomo had already begun to play its part in the public life of the city. The funeral of Filippo Visconti, the last of his lineage, was conducted there in 1447. And in 1450, Francesco Sforza visited the cathedral as his first public act to give thanks to the heavenly powers for having granted him the dukedom of Milan. Public enthusiasm for the event

Left, an engraving of 1808 showing the construction of the façade of the Duomo. At this time architects such as Soave, Pollak, Zanoia, and Amati were working on the cathedral. To the right in the engraving is the palace. The viceroy's carriage is emerging from the front of the royal residence.

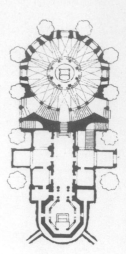

Right, plan of the crypt and the underground chapel where the body of Saint Carlo Borromeo lies.

Above, a nineteenth-century engraving of the Duomo and the piazza. The print shows the provisional wooden door that remained in the central portal until 1906, when Ludovico Pogliaghi's bronze door was installed.

Right, a longitudinal section through the Duomo.

was so great that he was rushed into the church while still on horseback.

Duke Francesco (1401–1466) had little patience with the Fabbrica which, he soon discovered, was quick to ask for privileges, favors, and donations but was extremely unwilling to accept criticism. Besides, styles of architecture were changing, and the new duke was in complete sympathy with the principles of the Renaissance. In his eagerness to turn Milan into a model Renaissance city, he lost interest in building the Duomo.

In the late fifteenth century, there was a renewal of interest in the cathedral. It was determined that the cathedral needed a cupola. The familiar disputes between experts and local builders recommenced. The current duke, Ludovico il Moro, searched throughout Italy for a new architect. Even Leonardo da Vinci submitted several designs, but none of them was accepted. Finally, the commission was given to two competent, though hardly brilliant, local craftsmen—Giovanni Antonio Amadeo and Gian Giacomb Dolcebuono. More with a view to forestalling criticism from outside than from any lack of confidence in their ability, final approval of their plan was left to the Tuscan Luca Fancelli and the Sienese Francesco di Giorgio.

The architects set to work in 1490. Ten years later, the cupola was completed, with the exception of the crowning pinnacle. Amadeo and Dolcebuono had been trained as sculptors rather than architects, which may account for their flamboyance. Later builders followed their style of elaborate ornamentation, which has left the Duomo looking like an enormous wedding cake.

The completion of the cupola was the occasion of celebration in Milan. But in 1535, Spanish troops invaded the city, and the foreign occupation put an end to the festivities. In addition, the Fabbrica had its own troubles. Amadeo died in 1522, and years passed under various unremarkable directors. In 1567, responsibility for the Duomo finally passed to Pellegrino Pellegrini, a favorite of the Cardinal Carlo Borromeo. The cardinal, leader of the Counter Reformation, favored Classical façades and vehemently opposed artistic extravagance. He ordered that the architecture of the cathedral be purged of all foreign—that is, Gothic—elements and redecorated in a more restrained and seemly fashion. Accordingly, Pellegrini, whose convictions matched those of the cardinal, broke completely with the self-effacing practices of his Renaissance predecessors and made any number of Baroque additions that were quite out of keeping with the Gothic spirit of the Duomo.

Pellegrini was also responsible for beginning work on the façade, although he managed to build less than half of it. His departure spurred renewed debate between those who favored a return to the Gothic and those who preferred a Classical style.

By the mid-seventeenth century, pro-Gothic sentiment had won out. However, in 1671, the Spanish government in control of Milan temporarily put an end to this costly embellishment of the church. The only eighteenth-century additions to the cathedral were some statues and the slender, filigreed spire of the cupola. The spire was actually finished in 1769, although the idea appears in much earlier drawings. The gilt statue of the Virgin, the

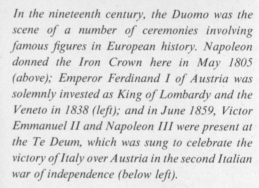

In the nineteenth century, the Duomo was the scene of a number of ceremonies involving famous figures in European history. Napoleon donned the Iron Crown here in May 1805 (above); Emperor Ferdinand I of Austria was solemnly invested as King of Lombardy and the Veneto in 1838 (left); and in June 1859, Victor Emmanuel II and Napoleon III were present at the Te Deum, which was sung to celebrate the victory of Italy over Austria in the second Italian war of independence (below left).

beloved *Madonnina,* was placed on the spire five years later.

After dragging on for centuries, construction of the cathedral was finally completed swiftly and efficiently in 1813 by order of Napoleon Bonaparte.

The massive Duomo takes the form of a Latin cross about 500 feet long and 300 feet wide at the transept. Inside and out, the cathedral is decorated with stone carvings, including more than three thousand statues. The façade is the most elaborately decorated section of the Duomo. Pilasters, statues, spires, arches, bronze doors, stone tassels, turrets, and intricate windows—a wealth of imaginative detail—merge into an overwhelming impression of voluptuous riches.

The Duomo rises 350 feet from ground level to the *Madonnina* atop the cupola. The marble roof, which was converted

into a terrace during the nineteenth century, ascends in easy, nearly flat, stages and is flanked by a forest of spires and statues. At the turn of the century, it was a popular refuge from the summer heat.

The interior of the cathedral is, in its way, as elaborate as the pointed, pierced, buttressed exterior. But the atmosphere is one of lofty decorum. The broad nave is flanked by four side aisles, each entered through a separate bronze door in the façade. Mighty columns, adorned with statues of the saints, culminate overhead in graceful, pointed arches.

Though huge in scale, the plan of the interior shows a striking simplicity, with few of the side chapels and monuments typical of traditional Gothic cathedrals. The ascetic Cardinal Borromeo swept away many of the early carvings and monuments that had encrusted the interior of the church. Much of the interior decoration that exists today is Baroque in style, the work of Borromeo's architect Pellegrini. Both the canopied high altar and the choir stalls are by Pellegrini. Beneath the choir is a crypt, also built by Pellegrini. This consists of the large winter

chapter house under the apse and a small chapel under the crossing. In the chapel lies the body of Saint Carlo Borromeo in a silver coffin commissioned by Philip IV of Spain. The glorious vaulted ceiling of the chapter house and the coffin are an ironic comment upon the asceticism espoused by the saint whose remains they glorify.

The design of the Duomo and its history are characterized by contradictions. The cathedral was built in a style both spiritually and geographically foreign to the city of Milan, by workmen unsympathetic to the principles of its design, through ages in which the original inspiration was gradually corrupted and lost. The completed Duomo belies the Gothic spirit in

Above, an early nineteenth-century view of the Duomo and the Piazzatta Reale that lies to the south of the cathedral.

which it was conceived. Begun at a time when Milan was proud and independent, the Duomo was completed, in the end, by order of a foreign conqueror.

But these contradictions contribute directly to the richness of the Duomo and its heritage. Because of them the cathedral remains a joyous and beloved landmark, one that is unequivocally unique.

Right, a picturesque view of the little lake at the Ospedale Maggiore, which existed well into the nineteenth century. Here, barges unloaded the marble from Candoglia that was used to build the Duomo. The Candoglia quarry was a gift to the Fabbrica from Gian Galeazzo Visconti. In return, the Fabbrica maintained the canals and waterways of the region.

Kandarya Mahadeva

India

Preceding page, the Kandarya Mahadeva, the greatest and most renowned of the eighty temples in the vast complex of Khajuraho. This city flourished during the tenth and eleventh centuries A.D. under the Candella dynasty. The contours of the temple are modeled on Mount Kailasa, the Himalayan peak revered as the dwelling of Shiva. The pyramid itself symbolizes the mountain top where the god resides with his shakti, the female divinity who complements him.

The exterior of the Kandarya Mahadeva is composed of multiple layers of cornices and staggered projections. The basic structural element of the temple is the square, the Hindu image of the universe.

The walls of the temple are embellished with a profusion of intricate carvings. The lower levels carry friezes of stylized figures of gods and god-kings in erotic conjunction with their consorts. The higher reaches bear lacy, geometric designs.

In these details, pairs of heavenly lovers who cover the walls of the temple engage in endlessly varied sexual conjunctions. Surasundari, *female celestial beings, stand attendant on every side. Their half-closed eyes and swaying stances express divine felicity.*

The halls leading to the inner sanctuary are ornamented with rich carvings and decorative elements on different levels (facing page and left). The sanctuary proper held the statue of the principal divinity as well as those of other gods and goddesses (below). Practically inaccessible, it was reserved for the priests and the sovereign, while the faithful thronged the pavilions and porticoes at the outer reaches of the temple.

Following page, detail of the splendid façade of the Kandarya Mahadeva.

Kandarya Mahadeva India

On the friezes of the Kandarya Mahadeva, the largest and most splendid of Khajuraho's thirty-five temples, lovers couple and intertwine with erotic abandon. The uninitiated visitor to this temple in India would probably only see wild sensuality; the observer well versed in Hinduism would perceive the supreme expression of Hindu philosophy in artistic form. Without any previous knowledge of Hinduism or Indian art, the Westerner is likely to misinterpret the explicit eroticism of the temple and miss its pervasive spiritual dimension. Yet, for the Hindus, who built the Kandarya Mahadeva, the artistic depiction of passion was neither unseemly nor profane. Rather, it was imbued with mystical meaning.

The Kandarya Mahadeva was built around A.D. 1000 by the reigning Candella dynasty (ca. 950–1050). During the height of their power, the Candellas raised eighty sanctuaries at Khajuraho, the holy city of their empire situated near the middle of northern India in Madhya Pradesh. Hindus from all reaches of the empire traveled to Khajuraho to worship the Trimurti, or Hindu trinity, which encompasses Brahma, soul and creator of the universe; Vishnu, the preserver; and Shiva, destroyer and re-creator.

All early Indian art is religious. The artist is not just a master craftsman. His sacred role is to mediate between the unfathomable realm of the divine and the visible world. The spiritual lies beyond rational understanding, but through deep, inspired meditation, the mind can transcend the physical world and, through ecstasy, comprehend the essence of god. The artist's task, which becomes a ritual act, is to translate these ecstatic intuitions into tangible images.

The Kandarya Mahadeva, dedicated to Shiva (Mahadeva), is an embodiment of Tantric doctrine. Basically, this belief states that a holy place must imitate the appearance of the created universe. Thus, the Kandarya Mahadeva resembles the sacred Mount Kailasa, the Hindu equivalent of Olympus. The temple must also provide a setting where the worshiper can approach and symbolically unite with the principal deity of the shrine.

The erotic imagery of the temple is also symbolic of Tantric teaching. Unlike most Western philosophies, the Tantra does not distinguish between the material body and the ethereal soul that dwells within. In-

Top and left, a plan and elevation of the temple. Above, Vishnu depicted in a circle with flames marking the cardinal points of the universe.

stead, it views body and soul as indivisible parts of a single, integral being. In the language of the Tantric symbols, the generative power of divinity takes male form, while human nature—with its receptivity to infusions from the divine—assumes the form of woman. Thus, sexual congress is symbolically equivalent to the rapture of the divine union. In this sense, nothing is closer to godliness than sexual ecstasy.

The composition and ground plan of the temple reflect religious belief no less

Above, a Western depiction of Shiva. He is shown with his traditional attributes—the third eye, the wheel, the battle-ax, the drum, and the necklace of severed heads—but also a violin, an unmistakably European import. The heads are all of white men.

Right, Shiva and Uma, one of his many wives. She is the daughter of the Himalayas and personifies the feminine principle. According to the doctrine of shaktism, the universe is the product of the male generative power—symbolized by the god—that is expressed through the female divinities who are his wives.

than the sensuous, exuberant figures that crowd its walls. Hindus envision the universe as a square, fashioned by divine hands from primeval chaos. An ancient Hindu text, the Rig-Veda, says:

> Long ago something nameless
>   hovered vast and unformed.
> It dimmed earth and heaven.
> The gods saw it and seized it.
> They dashed it to earth face
>   downward.
> They cast it to earth and they
>   sustain it.
> Brahma let the gods possess it,
>   and named it *vastu purusha.*

So *vastu purusha* is the name for "universe," and it has a form determined by the gods and approved by Brahma—the square. Because the temple is considered to be a microcosm of the universe, it embodies *vastu-purusha-mandala*, which, roughly translated, expresses the concept of "form in which being exists." Therefore, the temple is a faithful representation of the laws and principles that govern the entire cosmos and all of mankind—human existence being subject to cosmic law.

The architecture of the temples was entrusted to the priests. In Hindu thought, the architect was the agent through which anarchic elements were transformed into architectural structures that harmonized with the divine order. Every particle of every building—from the emperor's capital to the poorest hermitage—exemplified the coherent form into which chaotic material elements had been forced by divine power channeled through the architect. Indian temples are thus a strict arrangement of a series of square forms arranged on top of and within each other.

The nucleus of the ancient Hindu temple of northern India is the small, dark cell called the *garbha-griha*, its "holy of holies" buried deep within the building. In larger temples, this cubic space is surrounded by massive walls so that it becomes a kind of a cave at the heart of an architectural "mountain." The walls generally rise in a tower that is higher than it is wide. To this artificial mountain is added a second, au-

of the *lingam* was the center of the cult of Shiva, god of both regeneration and destruction. Complex fertility rituals, which appear to be patently exotic to the uninitiated, were based on the Hindu belief in the inseparability and integrity of body and soul. According to this belief, the conjoining of bodies is identical to the interpenetration of souls.

The seemingly unending friezes of *mithuna*—pairs of embracing lovers—on the outside of the temple are expressions of this Hindu cult of fertility. Even the main elements of the temple are symbolic: The tall, projecting *sikhara* and the low, broad *mukhashala* stand for the bridegroom and the bride of the Trimurti.

A common fertility rite involved the small golden box that the Hindus called the "seed" of the temple. The shape of this

tonomous architectural body: the *mukhashala,* a meeting hall that appeared regularly in temples after the eighth century. Its walls are much less massive than those of the *garbha-griha.* According to religious law, the entrance to the *mukhashala* faces east, and the windows opening to the light face north and south. The dark *garbha-griha* is entered through the western wall of the *mukhashala.*

The Kandarya Mahadeva of Khajuraho follows the classic architectural arrangement but with its own unique elaborations. Above the cell rises the traditional *sikhara,* a great tower with the outline typically associated with Hindu temples. Adhering to this, as though in bas-relief, are dozens of lesser towers that echo its form and structure.

Another departure from the strict classic design at the Kandarya Mahadeva is the *pradakshina patha,* the inner corridor or ambulatory where the faithful could pass in meditation before entering the sanctuary within. Its walls, like those on the outside, are stunningly and abundantly adorned. Inside is the *garbha-griha,* the "womb of the world" that contains the *lingam,* the great phallic symbol of the divine power of generation.

At Khajuraho as elsewhere, the worship

Above, the phallic lingam, *which represents Shiva in his aspect of the generative and recreative principle of the universe. This Western illustration, depicting the worshipers in the inauthentic posture of prostration, portrays a gross misunderstanding of Hindu philosophy.*

Below left, a bronze statuette of a bodhisattva, an enlightened soul who foregoes nirvana out of compassion for human misery. Below, a statue of Shiva, god of destruction and regeneration.

Above, Surya, god of the sun. He is traditionally accompanied by the charioteer Aruna in a seven-horse chariot, from which rays stream through the sky like arrows. Right, Candra, god of the moon, riding in his celestial car. Far right, an ivory plaque showing Rati, shakti *of the god of love.*

box, like the ground plan and rising patterns of the temple, was determined by *vastu-purusha-mandala.* The box contained the *mandala,* or model of the cosmos, subdivided by gold strips into smaller squares. The outer squares held lotus flowers, wheat, pigments, and metals. And the central square contained jewels and the symbolic attributes of the god. The seed, enclosing the forms of created nature, was imbedded into the temple wall on an "immaculate" or auspicious night.

Many other fertility rituals were observed during the construction of the tem-

ple. The choice of the site was preceded by elaborate ceremonies, performed by laborers under priestly supervision. And according to ancient Hindu texts, once the plans for a temple had been completed, the architects were sacrificed and entombed in the foundations.

The Tantrists generally established their holy places in remote locations. The sanctuary of Konarak, for example, is built on sand dunes by the Bay of Bengal. They realized that their religion—especially with its obvious sensuality—could easily be misunderstood or misused. But

since Khajuraho was a capital city of an empire, it was never isolated and is easily accessible today.

In fact, the Kandarya Mahadeva has become the principal attraction of a tourist village that has grown up in the eastern section of the ancient city. The stream of Hindu worshipers has all but ceased, but ironically, the temple has more visitors today than ever in its history. Travelers and connoisseurs from around the globe converge at the temple to delight in the lithe power of its carvings and to study the beauty of the temple as a whole.

Facing page, the central nave, dominated by the vertical lines of its clustered pilasters, looking toward the Baroque high altar (this page, left). Above, a Gothic altar embellished with Baroque detail. Below right, elaborate Baroque altars flanking the columns in the nave. Below left, the fifteenth-century Schutzmantel Madonna which adorns one of the columns in the nave.

In the façade the Gothic structure appears to have been grafted onto existing Romanesque remains, but elsewhere the cathedral displays the highly elaborate Gothic style of the fourteenth and fifteenth centuries.

Left, a gable over one of the two entrances to the nave, located behind the façade chapels. (The Giant's Doorway in the western façade is opened only on important occasions.)

Below left, Gothic statuary, based on historical and secular rather than Biblical characters, and below right, the Baroque statue of Saint Francis.

The Gothic spirit of the cathedral is exemplified by the Steffe, the southern bell tower seen above the choir roof in the foreground (facing page). The imposing bulk of the roof is somewhat lightened by the diamond design of the colored tiles.

Preceding page, the spired bell tower and sharply pitched roof of the Cathedral of St. Stephen dominating the Viennese skyline. The cathedral was begun in the thirteenth century and finished in the fifteenth.

Facing page, the lower façade, which bears the most clear traces of the previous Romanesque church. The image of Christ the Pancreator, set above the Giant's Doorway (Riesentor), is a classic Romanesque motif.

Right, one of the rose windows restored after World War II. It is set into one of the Gothic chapels which were added on either side of the façade (below).

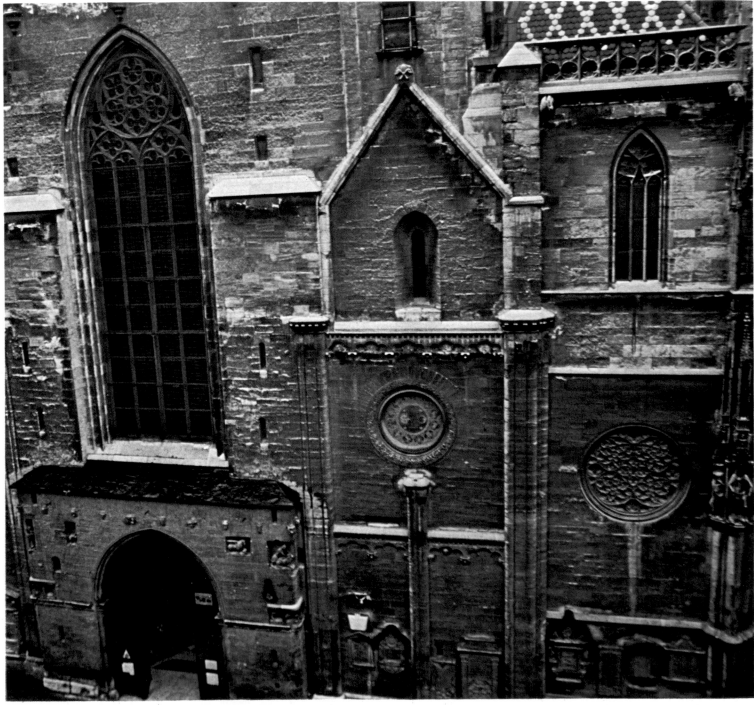

St. Stephen's

Austria

Facing page, above, figures of Saint Barbara (left), the Virgin (center), and Saint Catherine (right) on the Wiener-Neustädter altar. Below, two of the many Baroque altars in the nave.

This page, views of the pulpit. A masterpiece of Flamboyant Gothic, it is remarkable for two self-portraits of its creator, Anton Pilgram, who with architect's diviners in hand, peers out from the base of the pulpit (above).

Following page, St. Stephen's overlooking the Vienna Woods.

St. Stephen's Austria

The Cathedral of St. Stephen, the principal church of Vienna, stands at the heart of Viennese life and has held a dominant place in the history of the city. In the days before newspapers, the proclamations of emperors, archbishops, and popes were posted on its massive door. From the cathedral's steeple, sentries watched the outlying areas for invaders; and its great bell, cast in the early eighteenth century, became the voice of the city. For centuries the Viennese have gathered before St. Stephen's in times of trouble and joy, as they still do today.

The exalted cathedral grew from humble beginnings. Christianity had been practiced in Vienna since the last days of the Roman Empire, when Vienna was a small town clustered around the fortified camp of the Roman conquerors. By the twelfth century, the former imperial outpost had grown into a rich and prosperous city. It was designated the capital of the Eastern Kingdom, or Ostarrichi, from which was derived the name "Österreich," as Austria is known in modern German. Since the ancient, walled city was no longer large enough to contain the expanding population, Vienna's boundaries were extended, and in 1147, work began on the first Church of St. Stephen—a large Romanesque basilica within the new walls.

The idea for a church was at least partially attributable to the civic and political foresight of the eighth margrave (lord or military commander) von Babenberg, whose family ruled Austria from the ninth to the twelfth century. The margrave recognized that a strong church was a basic prerequisite of a ducal city. In a sense, the erection of the church predicted the destiny of the city, for in 1156, the margrave did obtain the title of duke.

The basilica eventually became the main parish church of Vienna, but it remained dependent on the Bishop of Passau, who allowed the church to use the name of Saint Stephen—the first Christian martyr.

A hundred years later, however, a new basilica was constructed on the site by Ottokar II of Bohemia. Ottokar had seized the city in 1251 after five years of anarchy, triggered by the death of Frederick II, last of the Babenbergs.

There were numerous reasons for the new building. The original church had been badly damaged by fire, first in 1193 and again in 1258. Another reason may have been the desire of the newly rich middle class for a more prestigious church; apart from Cologne, Vienna had become the leading German-speaking city. The city was a flourishing commercial

Left, an engraving of the Heiltumsstuhl ("the seat of holy things") where the holy relics of the cathedral were displayed on holy days. Below, a plan showing the evolution of the cathedral from the tenth to the sixteenth centuries. Right, the south façade of the church in an engraving by Solomon Kleiner.

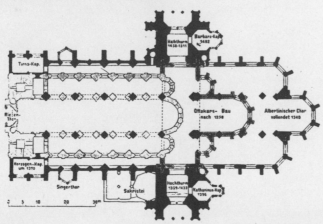

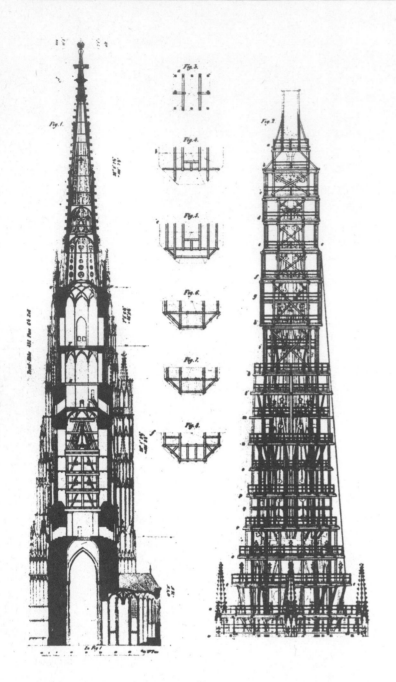

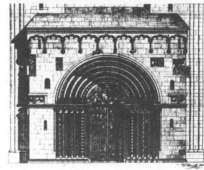

Far left, a cross section of the bell tower and a design for scaffolding to surround the steeple. Left, the Giant's Doorway. Above, St. Stephen's as depicted by Karl Schutz in 1792.

center on the Danube, standing at the crossroads of the important trade routes between Venice and the northern Slavic and Baltic countries and between Western Europe and the East.

The new church, completed about 1267, was slightly larger than its predecessor. But because Ottokar II failed to persuade the bishop to relinquish such a lucrative part of his seat, St. Stephen's remained a parish church belonging to the diocese of Passau.

In the thirteenth century, the years of economic expansion were just beginning for Vienna, bringing a surge of building activity. The Hapsburgs were primarily responsible for both developments, beginning in 1276 when Rudolf of Hapsburg

dispossessed Ottokar of his Austrian provinces. The following year Rudolf recognized Vienna as a free imperial city—a semiautonomous city-state within the empire—that had special commercial rights. Yet, despite economic and social advances at this time, Vienna was culturally isolated from the rest of Europe. Even as the city of Cologne was demolishing its Romanesque church to erect a Gothic one, Vienna went on using the Romanesque style.

Rudolf still wished to exercise some control over the city, and he intermittently succeeded in having his way. But by 1288, the Viennese had devised a solid, municipal government presided over by a burgomaster. Some of Rudolf's successors were even less willing than he had been to

grant the city full autonomy, even attempting to impose severe limitations. But it was not easy to revoke an independence once given, and Vienna remained a free city until 1526.

Under the liberal rule of the Hapsburgs, the merchant class once again turned to St. Stephen's as a symbol of their emerging pre-eminence. In 1304, the land around the apse of the church was purchased, and building was begun on a great choir and a new apse. By this time, the Gothic had reached Vienna, introduced by the Cistercians, a monastic order which had originated in France.

In the early fourteenth century, St. Stephen's was slowly transformed from a Romanesque to a Gothic church. Only the

Right, two cross sections through the west end of the nave showing the structure of the vaulting and the original timber roof. Below right, the façade of St. Stephen's in a nineteenth-century engraving.

west front, with its Giant's Doorway (Riesentor) and the two Heathens' Towers (Heidenturme), was preserved; and from 1304 to 1450, the 360-foot-long Gothic structure rose inexorably behind it. Why the west façade was left intact is unknown, although it might have been because the church had become a symbol of the city as well as the recipient of frequent donations from Christians hoping to procure a place in Heaven. At any rate, when plans were begun for the Gothic reconstruction of the building, it was apparently never even suggested that the ancient façade be changed.

The foundation stone of the new building was laid on April 7, 1357, by Duke Rudolf IV of Hapsburg. (A statue of the duke, wearing a crown and carrying a model of the church in his hand, still stands in a side niche.) Rudolf fully understood the political significance of the new church. In 1364, he and his brothers signed a reciprocal agreement that committed them to active work on the church until it was completed. Unfortunately, Rudolf died the same year in Milan, at the age of twenty-six. At this time, work on the towers was about to begin. Only the south one was ever built, and even so, it was not completed until the fifteenth century. The architect Hans von Prachatitz eventually finished the tower in 1433, and Hans Puchsbaum was responsible for vaulting the central nave during the years 1440 to 1455.

After the death of Rudolf, the Austrian dukes, despite their solemn vow, neglected the church. Work progressed only on account of the continued dedication and financial support of the populace. And in 1469, St. Stephen's was at last confirmed by the pope as a bishop's see. Ironically, the enhanced rank of the church did not hasten its construction. Work on the cathedral proceeded fitfully and ceased altogether in 1511.

At this time the church was essentially finished, apart from the completion of the second bell tower. Despite its hundreds of indentations, niches, and openings, the church retains a superb unity. The roofs are steeply pitched to prevent the accumulation of snow. In the absence of flying buttresses, the steepness of the roofs and the colored tiles in zigzag patterns give St. Stephen's that soaring upthrust characteristic of the Gothic style. The entire structure is crowned by the slender arrow of the bell tower.

Within the cathedral, the chancel, although it is smaller in scale than the nave, serves as the dramatic focus of the church, owing to a combination of unusual architectural relationships. The bell tower and its unfinished twin are situated between the nave and the chancel and form a pseudotransept. They thus symbolically separate the area occupied by the congregation from that once occupied by the clergy in the chancel, or choir. As in some English Gothic churches and—following the example of St. Stephen's—some other Austrian churches, the vaults of the chancel of St. Stephen's are lower than those in the nave. This is because the chancel was built to the scale of the old nave, although in the new style. When the nave itself was updated a century later, it was rebuilt on a much larger scale, thus altering the customary spatial relationships between the chancel and nave.

In the apse of the south aisle, Emperor Frederick III is entombed in a monumental sarcophagus of red marble. The sarcophagus is only one among many celebrated works of sculpture that adorn both the exterior and interior of the cathedral. One of the most interesting is the *Madonna of the Maidservants*. A fine example of fourteenth-century sculpture, this statue is also the subject of a strange legend. A long time ago, so the story goes, the statue was owned by a rich woman who kept it in her bedchamber. While dressing for a ball one night, she discovered that her most precious ring was missing. The police were called in, and the lady contemptuously accused the maid, who flung herself at the feet of the Madonna and prayed desper-

Above, a painting of St. Stephen's by Rudolf von Alt. The square served as a meeting place for the 600,000 inhabitants of the imperial city.

ately for help. The servant was nonetheless hauled to her feet and bound in chains. As the lady prepared to abandon the poor girl to her fate, she put on a glove—and found the missing ring in the tip of a finger. In the ensuing confusion, it was decided to donate the statue to the cathedral. The Madonna now stands on an altar once used for morning prayer by domestics on their way to work, and since the time of the legend, generations of maids have knelt in front of the statue to relate the cruelties of their mistresses.

In the early sixteenth century, the threat of Lutheran reform and the Turkish menace curtailed religious building in Vienna. Fortifications were the order of the day. But the Viennese got their revenge in 1683, when the second and last great Turkish invasion was thrown back from their gates. With the cannons that they captured from the enemy, the citizens of Vienna made the great bell called Pummering, and its tolling soon became a familiar and beloved sound throughout the city.

Some three hundred years later, St. Stephen's was again threatened. The church was badly damaged during World War II. From March 23 to April 13, 1945, Vienna was the scene of a terrible battle between

German and Russian troops, and the retreating German commander is said to have turned his guns on the city. The cathedral roof burned and vaulting over the choir collapsed, destroying the Gothic choir stalls, the rood screen, and the twenty-ton Pummering bell.

But as early as Christmas of 1948, the central nave was restored, and the citizens once more were able to gather to sing the carol *Stille Nacht*. Pummering was recast and the roof redecorated with glazed ceramic tiles as before, but this time they were mounted on a framework of steel.

St. Stephen's is both a monument and historic landmark. Emperors, princes, and archbishops are buried within its walls, and at one time, it was even the burial place of the poor and victims of the plague.

The great cathedral speaks for the nation each New Year's Eve, when radios all over Austria are tuned to Vienna to hear Pummering toll the changing year. In a tradition that combines national pride and religious affirmation, the Viennese begin each year with a solemn blessing from the steeple of St. Stephen's.

Westminster Abbey

Preceding page, an aerial view of the abbey. Westminster was originally the church of a large Benedictine monastery that gave its name (West Minster) to what had been known as Thorney Island. The island has since been absorbed into the north bank of the Thames.

Left, the west or main façade of the abbey, seen from Victoria Street. In the distance is the Victoria Tower of the Houses of Parliament.

Below left, the exterior of the Chapel of Henry VII attached to the east end of the abbey.

Right, details of the buttresses of the abbey.

Facing page, the two great towers on the west façade of the abbey. Though the church was consecrated in 1269, the towers were not added until the eighteenth century. Begun in 1722 by Christopher Wren, they were completed by Nicholas Hawksmoor in 1745. The newer work blends well enough with the original Gothic, though the towers are of Portland stone and are much lighter in color than the lower part of the abbey. The façade itself was also modified by Hawksmoor.

Right, the north side or left side of the west front. This tower contains the belfry of the abbey.

Above, the Houses of Parliament. The name Westminster is no longer famous for its association with the abbey alone. It is also synonymous with the Houses of Parliament, the various ministries situated nearby— indeed, the government itself—as well as the local metropolitan district. Parliament originally met in the chapter house of the abbey and moved across the road to its present site during the reign of Henry VIII. Most of the present Parliament buildings date from the nineteenth century, after a fire destroyed the earlier buildings. The oldest surviving part of the ancient Palace of Westminster is Westminster Hall (seen at left), a royal banquet hall that dates almost as far back as the Norman Conquest. The massive Victoria Tower (seen at right) holds the archives of Parliament, where the original copy of every act of Parliament since 1497 is kept.

Facing page and above left and right, views of the Great Cloister. The cloisters link parts of the complex, such as the church, the chapter house, and the refectory. They also served as places of work and recreation as well as of spiritual peace and contemplation.

Below right, a view from the deanery looking north toward the abbey's south tower.

Below, a gate in the corner of the Little Dean's Yard.

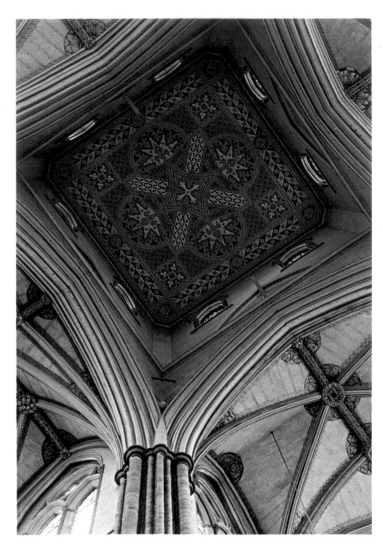

There is a dramatic contrast between the still somewhat French Gothic of the abbey itself (facing page, above left), seen in the crossing and the western part of the nave (above right), and the magnificent, early sixteenth-century fan vaulting (below) in the east end of the Chapel of Henry VII.

This page, below, a view down the nave of the abbey toward the apse showing the early nineteenth-century choir screen. Visible over the screen (above) are the pipes of the organ. Below right, the restored rose window in the south transept.

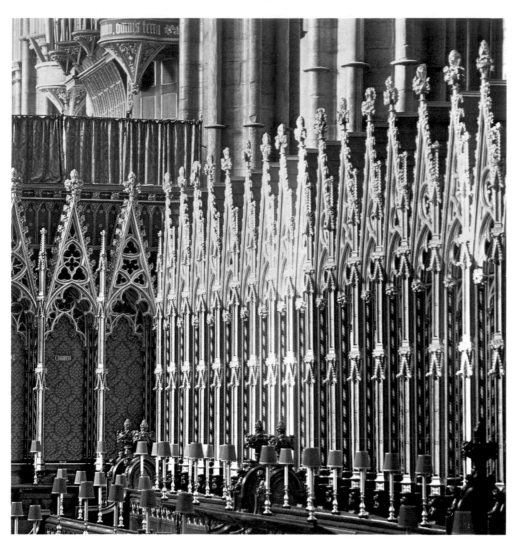

Left and below, the choir stalls. The original choir stalls dating from the thirteenth century were destroyed in 1775; the present ones, the work of Edward Blore, were made in 1847.

Facing page, three statues in a small side chapel to the right of the Chapel of Henry VII. They represent, from left to right: Saint Clare holding a pyx, Saint Roch with a dog, and Saint Monica with a small vase.

The Chapel of Henry VII—"the loveliest jewel of Christendom"—is a small, virtually self-contained church attached to the east end of the abbey. Built between 1503 and 1519, it contains the tombs of Tudor and Stuart monarchs. The standards above the choir stalls bear the coats of arms of the knights of the Order of the Bath. In the chapel is a memorial to the men of the Royal Air Force killed during the Battle of Britain.

Facing page, the western end of the chapel. Below, the choir stalls. Right, the fan-vaulted ceiling at the east end of the chapel. Above, detail of the stone pendant in the center of the ceiling.

Two views of the coronation chair are shown on this page. Commissioned by Edward I, it sits atop the legendary Stone of Scone. This stone, traditionally used during the coronation of Scottish kings, was captured from Scone Abbey by Edward I and brought back to London as a trophy. The chair has been used for the coronation of every British monarch since 1296, except for Edward V and Edward VIII, who were never formally crowned.

Facing page, views of the Chapel of St. Paul in the ambulatory of the abbey. The tomb of Ludovic Robsart, Lord Bouchier, is incorporated into the stone screen of the chapel. Of Flemish birth, he fought against the French at the Battle of Agincourt and is said to have been Henry V's standard-bearer. He died in 1431.

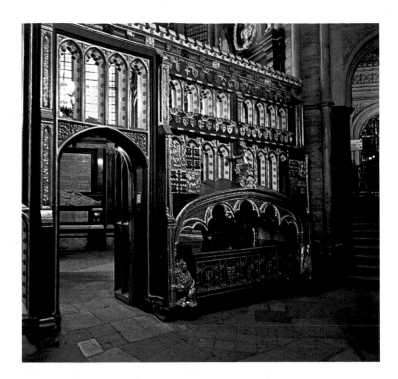

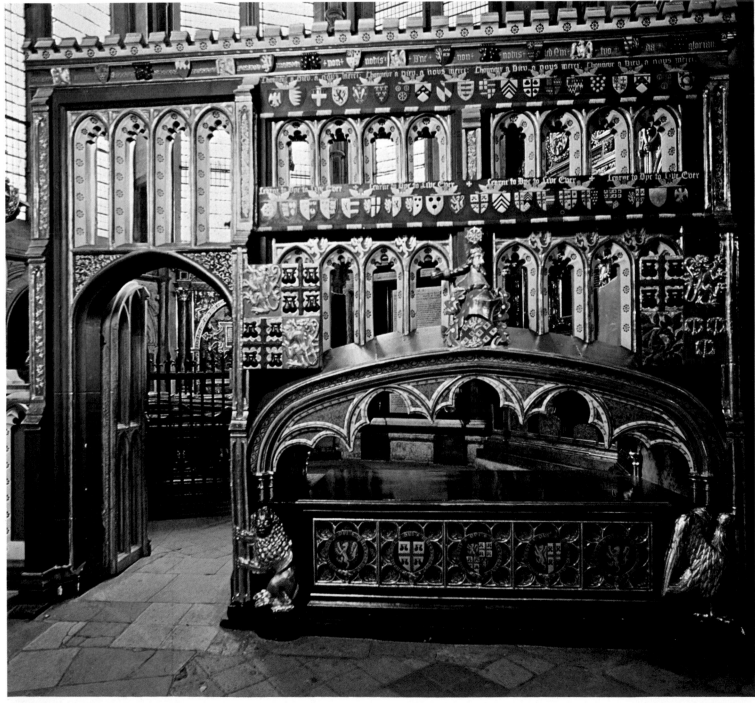

Facing page, the pulpit of the abbey, which dates from the early seventeenth century.

Right, with detail below, the Renaissance-style bronze tomb effigies of Henry VII and his queen, Elizabeth of York. In the middle of the Chapel of Henry VII, they contrast with their Gothic surroundings and the Gothic screen that encloses them. The effigies, made between 1512 and 1518, are the work of a Florentine, Pietro Torrigiano.

Many English sovereigns were buried in the abbey, up to the time of George II. Above, Henry III. Above left, one of the "Weepers"—his children—from the tomb of Richard III. Left, Henry V, Shakespeare's Prince Hal. Originally, Henry's wooden effigy had a head and hands of silver, but these were stolen centuries ago. They were replaced quite recently with carvings of polyester resin.

Facing page, the tomb of Elizabeth I. Created by Maximilian Colt and John de Critz, it stands in the Chapel of Henry VII. The tomb also holds her half sister, Mary I (known as Bloody Mary), who was as staunchly Catholic as Elizabeth was Protestant.

GEORGE FREDERICK HANDEL Esq.
born February XXIII MDCLXXXIV.
died April XIV. MDCCLIX.
L.F.Roubiliac inv.t et sc.t

THOMAS STEARNS ELIOT OM

ALFRED
LORD TENNYSON.
BORN
AUGUST 6 1809.
DIED
OCTOBER 6 1892.

ROBERT
BROWNING
MAY 7 1812
DEC 12 1889

Facing page, the graves of Browning, Tennyson, and the American-born T. S. Eliot (below); an austere monument to Shakespeare (far left); and a Baroque monument to the composer Handel (left), all in Poet's Corner in the south transept. Although Handel is commemorated here, most of the musicians are in the north aisle of the nave.

Right, the monument to Thomas Thynne in the south aisle of the nave. It depicts his murder in 1682 at the hands of highwaymen hired by Count Hans Christoph Königsmark who wanted Thynne's bride.

Center, monument to Major John André, who was accused of having been a spy for the British during the American Revolution. André was executed by the Americans in 1780. The monument shows George Washington receiving André's petition.

Below right, in the north transept, the monument to Sir Francis Vere, who died in 1609.

Below, Roubillac's dramatic monument showing Lady Elizabeth Nightingale struck down by Death. She died in 1731 from a miscarriage brought on by her fear of a lightning storm.

The façade of Westminster Abbey (following page) took centuries to complete. The upper parts of the towers were built in the eighteenth century by the architect Nicholas Hawksmoor, who successfully integrated his work with the original Gothic style of the abbey.

Westminster Abbey England

The earliest history of Westminster Abbey, like the history of England itself, is shrouded in myth and legend. One story holds that Lucius, a British king of the second century A.D., built a Christian church where the abbey stands today. Another claims that the Saxon King Sebert, who died early in the seventh century, founded a church on that spot. The legend favoring Sebert also maintains that the church was consecrated by Saint Peter himself. Indeed, until the fourteenth century, local fishermen brought an annual tribute of salmon to the monks of the abbey in honor of the holy fisherman.

It is only known for certain that a Saxon monastic church, dating from at least 750, was erected on Thorney Island in the Thames. The church stood near the site of the present abbey on the foundations of a much older Roman building. Some two hundred years later, the monastery was enlarged and reorganized by Saint Dunstan, the Archbishop of Canterbury, who helped spread Christianity throughout England.

Westminster Abbey itself was founded a century later by the pious Edward the Confessor, second to last of England's line of Saxon kings. Near the existing building, he constructed a new and richly endowed monastery with a church, modeled after the abbey churches of Normandy. The abbey was all but finished late in the year 1065 and was consecrated just a few weeks before his death.

Edward the Confessor, as his appellation suggests, was attracted more to the spiritual than to the secular life. Though he married the daughter of the powerful Earl Godwin, he lived apart from his wife for many years and produced no heirs. As Edward grew older, he gradually withdrew into monkish seclusion. Eventually, he willingly permitted the Godwins to govern the country, while he remained king in name only. No one knows for certain whether Edward actually left his kingdom to his brother-in-law Harold Godwinson or to his French cousin William, Duke of Normandy, also known as William the Bastard. Many years earlier Edward had made friendly overtures to William, but it is quite likely that, as he lay dying, the saintly king was preoccupied with matters other than the succession to the throne.

Upon Edward's death, Harold claimed the throne, and William immediately set out to seize what he believed to be rightfully his. He set sail for England and, on October 14, 1066, defeated Harold's army at Hastings in a battle which marked the

Above left, a miniature depicting the coronation of Henry III, who began building the Gothic abbey that stands today. Progress was slowed during a series of wars afflicting Henry's successors, including Richard II (above right). Right, a thirteenth-century woodcut depicting a group of builders.

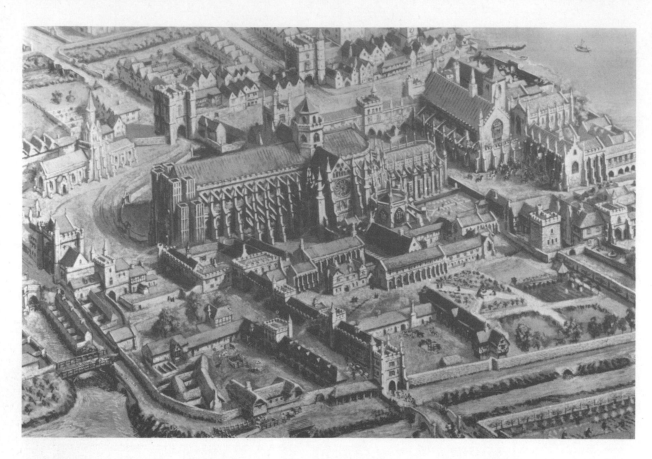

Left, a reconstruction of the area around the abbey as it was in the sixteenth century. At that time, the towers of the west front had not yet been added.

Below, a procession of knights in front of Westminster in a painting by Canaletto.

last invasion of England by a foreign army. William the Bastard thus became William the Conqueror.

The Normans promptly installed themselves at Westminster, and William had himself crowned at the abbey, inaugurating a tradition that continues to this day. The city of London, situated between the new king's court on the west and the great Tower he built on its east wall, was established as the heart of the new Norman kingdom.

The Confessor's church remained unaltered for two centuries. Then, in 1216, Henry III, a mere nine years old, ascended the throne. His qualities were the sort that endeared him more to later generations than to his contemporaries. Henry was the son of the hated King John, who had been forced by his subjects to sign the Magna Carta. Naturally enough, his father's experiences made Henry a cautious man. Although an indecisive king and a poor soldier, Henry was nevertheless a kindly man and a generous patron of the arts. He was eager to bring culture and, especially, architecture in England up to Continental standards of Gothic elegance.

Edward the Confessor had been canonized in 1163, and Henry III had placed himself under that saint's special protection. He decided to pull down Edward's old Norman church and erect in its place a splendid church in the Gothic style, to the greater glory of God, England, and the royal saint. Though the monastery buildings were left intact, and still exist in part,

the entire church was eventually demolished and a new one begun under his personal supervision. In fact, the king's master masons Elias and Henry answered only to the king. The mason Henry was known as Henry of Reyns, whose name undoubtedly derived from the town of Reims in France. Having admired the mighty cathedral there, King Henry wanted his own

Right, a portrait of Elizabeth I that is now in the National Maritime Museum in Greenwich.

church to be built in the style of the French Gothic. Consequently, Westminster, with its lofty vaulting, owes much to the High Gothic masterpieces at Reims and Amiens.

Laborers began demolishing the old church around 1243. The huge church erected in its place—the structure which still stands today—measures about 530 feet in length, 200 feet across at the transept, and 95 feet at the highest point of the nave. The ground plan, in the form of a Latin cross, is based on that of the previous abbey, but the dimensions are much greater. It follows the plan of a pilgrimage church. Aisles flank the nave and pass around the transepts, meeting behind the apse to form an ambulatory from which the royal chapels radiate. Moreover, since it is an abbey and not a cathedral, the church is the centerpiece of a complex that includes the chapter house, dormitories, and cloisters.

At the king's insistence, only the finest materials were used in the abbey, including Purbeck marble, stone from quarries at Reigate, and white stone brought across the English Channel from Caen. Despite Henry's eagerness to see the church completed, work proceeded slowly and was

still only partially finished when the abbey was consecrated in 1269. When Henry

died in 1272 after a long reign, the new building consisted only of the transepts, the chancel, and part of the nave. Most of the nave of the former church was to remain in use for another hundred years.

Although Henry did not have the pleasure of seeing his church finished, he was able to move the remains of Edward the Confessor into the gold and glass shrine he had made to hold them. The event took place, with great ceremony, on October 13, 1269.

The kings who succeeded Henry III took little interest in completing his church. It was not until 1375 that the architect Henry Yevele received the approval of his sovereign, Edward III, to finish the nave. And the twin towers that today seem to characterize the church are actually comparatively modern. Begun in 1722 by Christopher Wren, the towers were completed in 1745 following the de-

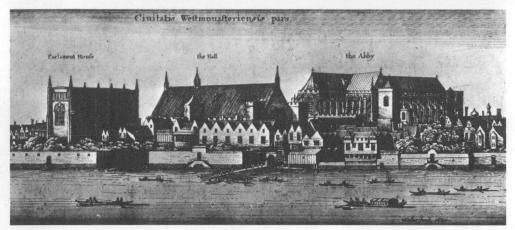

Left, the great courtyard of the Palace of West-minster, with the abbey looming in the distance. Below left, Westminster seen from the Thames. These illustrations date from the second half of the seventeenth century.

sign of Nicholas Hawksmoor. Constructed of the luminous Portland stone associated with Georgian London, they are lighter in color than the medieval body of the abbey, and there is something slightly artificial about their Gothic style.

For the most part, the rest of the construction that has taken place at Westminster Abbey has been in the nature of repair and restoration, with one exception—the exuberant, fan-vaulted Chapel of Henry VII, begun in 1505.

The lofty Gothic interior of Westminster Abbey refines and restates the cathedral architecture of France that Henry III so admired. The human interest of the abbey, however, lies not in its soaring vaults, galleries, or rose windows but much closer to eye level. Under the paving stones of the church, unceremoniously trodden by worshipers and tourists alike, lie the bones of the renowned and the wealthy—men, women, and children whose very names recall centuries of English history. Assorted memorials— from simple slabs to ornate shrines— crowd the stone walls and floors of

the church and fill its many chapels.

At the end of the nave just inside the west door, a stone surrounded by poppies is set into the floor. Here lies the Tomb of the Unknown Soldier, a nameless young man killed in France during World War I. His simple grave is a memorial to an entire generation of young Englishmen who died in that bloody and most senseless war.

The north aisle, mainly dedicated to politicians, holds the graves and memorials of several British prime ministers. Here is a huge allegorical monument to Charles James Fox, the British politician who supported the cause of the rebellious colonies during the American Revolution. Fox, dressed in a toga, is shown expiring on a couch. He is supported by a female Liberty, and a Negro at his feet commemorates Fox's role in the abolition of slavery in the British Empire. Nearby, over the west door, is a less imposing monument honoring Fox's rival William Pitt. Ironically, both men died in 1806 and are buried in the north transept of the abbey. There is also a plaque erected in memory of Franklin D. Roosevelt. Another notable

buried here is the poet and playwright Ben Jonson, who died in 1637.

One of the most interesting monuments in the south aisle is the one to Thomas Thynne, politician and nobleman of the time of George III, which depicts in relief his melodramatic end: He was slain by hired highwaymen in Pall Mall in 1682. Though most of the memorials in this aisle honor military men, the Methodist preacher John Wesley lies among them. The Restoration dramatist William Congreve is also buried here, and on the wall is a monument to Sir Godfrey Kneller, the only painter represented in the abbey. His body lies elsewhere, for he had once declared: "By God, I will not be buried in Westminster . . . . They do bury fools there."

At the heart of the abbey is the high altar, where coronations, royal weddings, and funerals are still celebrated. The altar is part of the sacrarium, or sanctuary. On the left side of the sacrarium, covered by beautiful stone canopies, are the three fourteenth-century tombs of Edmund Crouchback, Earl of Lancaster, his wife Aveline of Lancaster, and a cousin, Aymer de Valence.

The shrine of Saint Edward occupies a place of honor in the church, behind the altar. Only remnants of the tomb's gold and glass mosaic remain. The base of the marble tomb is Cosmati work signed "Pietrus Romano" and dated 1270. The base supports the two-storied catafalque of the Confessor. This ancient shrine, defaced and worn with age, nevertheless remains somber and majestic.

The mystical King Edward was credited by his subjects with the ability to cure illness with a touch, a belief that did not entirely die out until the eighteenth century. Up until that time, it was customary to leave the sick and ailing overnight in the pointed niches at the base of his tomb. Ironically, it is also said that, in 1413, King Henry IV was kneeling in one of these recesses when he fell fatally ill. The king was later carried to the Jerusalem Chamber, where he died.

Encircling the monument to the Confessor are the tombs of the Plantagenet kings and queens. Here is the canopied tomb of the warrior King Edward III, who died in 1377, and the tomb of his wife Philippa of Hainaut. A courageous and highly civilized woman who accompanied her husband on his military campaigns, Philippa is best remembered for having persuaded Edward to spare the lives of the six burghers of Calais who had surrendered themselves to him as hostages. Next to their tombs is that built by the grief-stricken Richard II for the remains of his beloved wife Anne of Bohemia. The effigy, carved when the king was still alive, shows the royal couple holding hands. Richard was deposed and murdered by Henry IV in 1399, and his remains were finally brought to the abbey to lie beside those of his queen in the reign of Henry V.

A simple marble monument encloses the tomb of Edward I. Next to it is the magnificent tomb of his father, Henry III, founder of the abbey. Henry's marble sarcophagus is decorated with slabs of porphyry, said to have been brought from Palestine by Edward I. Henry was moved to this resting place from a grave by the high altar in 1291. Eleanor of Castile, wife of Edward I, is also buried here. Her effigy, the work of the London goldsmith William Torel, is an actual portrait, which is unusual for its time.

Opposite Edward's shrine stands the coronation chair, on which all the monarchs of Great Britain since Edward I have been crowned. The chair is badly worn and carved with the names of long-dead tourists. Beneath it sits a gray rock—the legendary Stone of Scone. The stone, sacred to the Scots, had been used for centuries for the coronation of Scottish kings. Edward I, the Malleus Scotorum, or Hammer of the Scots, seized the stone and had it brought to Westminster in 1296. Evidently, Edward envisioned the stone as a dramatic symbol of his mastery over the Scots. However, Scotland remained rebellious—and independent—until King James

Left, portrait of Mary Queen of Scots, who was executed on February 8, 1587. Her body ultimately came to rest in Westminster Abbey in a magnificent monument James I raised to his mother.

Below, the coronation of Charles II at Westminster Abbey in 1661, at which time the monarchy was restored after the Commonwealth of Oliver Cromwell.

Left, a print dated 1793 of Westminster Abbey by B. Hall. St. Margaret's Church, built in the sixteenth century, is in the background.

Below left, the distant Gothic spires of Westminster Abbey forming a background for St. James' Park, a popular meeting place for king and courtiers in the eighteenth century.

Below, the solemn coronation of Queen Victoria in Westminster Abbey. During her reign from 1837 to 1901, England achieved worldwide power and prestige.

VI of Scotland was crowned James I of England in 1603. And even then, political union with England was not achieved until the reign of Queen Anne a century later.

The transepts of the abbey stretch north and south to end in two fine rose windows. In the north transept are white marble memorials to the foremost political figures of the nineteenth century. One of the abbey's most macabre displays also stands here—Roubillac's monument depicting the figure of Death taking fatal aim at Lady Elizabeth Nightingale, who swoons into her helpless husband's arms.

The south transept, affectionately known as Poet's Corner, is a virtual "Who's Who" of English literature. The earliest grave here is that of Chaucer, who died in 1400, although his canopied tomb was not erected until 1555. In 1599, Edmund Spenser was buried close by. Here is a pensive, cross-legged Shakespeare and, at his feet, the grave of the actor David Garrick. Here, too, are buried Tennyson and Browning, Samuel Johnson and Charles Dickens. Among the memorials are those to Dryden, Wordsworth, Coleridge, Longfellow, Thackeray, Keats, and Shelley. Most of the monuments to the early writers date from the eighteenth century, for prior to that, literature was not considered a particularly honorable profession.

Radiating from the ambulatory that winds around the apse are the royal chap-

Left, the abbey and the old Palace of Westminster, seen from Old Westminster Bridge in a print dated 1819.

els, resting places of the kings and queens of England and other aristocrats. The Chapel of St. Edmund contains one of the abbey's earliest monuments, the grave of William de Valence, Earl of Pembroke and half brother to Henry III, who died in 1296. His oak effigy is covered with gilded copper and bears a shield decorated with Limoges enamel work. Early members of the politically powerful Cecil family, marquises of Salisbury, are buried in the Chapel of St. Nicholas. The Percy family, dukes of Northumberland, still retains the right of burial in this chamber.

At the end of the apse, beyond the ambulatory is the Chapel of Henry VII, a magnificent addition to the main structure of the church. Henry VII was the founder of the House of Tudor, which reigned over one of the most glorious ages in English history. His reputation for stringent measures—based mostly on the efficient system of taxation he imposed on his subjects—is belied by the splendor of his chapel, which has been called "the loveliest jewel of Christendom."

Colorful heraldic banners of the knights of the Order of the Bath flank the fan-vaulted ceiling, a miracle of stone carving. The intricate network of delicate fans, with their stone pendants, forms a lacy canopy. If the ceiling is a joyous expression of the late Gothic, the bronze tomb below—with its noble effigies of Henry and his queen, Elizabeth of York, created by the Florentine sculptor Pietro Torrigiano—ushers in the English Renaissance. In another part of the chapel, which is actually a small church in itself, is an even greater work by Torrigiano—the serene and lifelike effigy of Lady Margaret Beaufort, the mother of Henry VII.

In the south aisle of the chapel stands the elaborate Jacobean tomb of Mary Queen of Scots; the north aisle contains the similar but somewhat less elaborate tomb of Elizabeth I. The snub is intentional, for the two monuments were erected by James I, whose mother, the Scottish queen, was beheaded on the orders of Elizabeth. Queen Elizabeth also shares her tomb with her half sister, the Catholic Queen Mary I, whom she succeeded. Mary is remembered as Bloody Mary on account of the religious persecution which took place during her reign, although in fact she was by nature gentle and merciful.

Several Stuart kings and queens are buried without memorial under the black and white marble floor. The chapel also holds the vault of King George II, last sovereign of England to be buried in the abbey, and a memorial to the men of the Royal Air Force who died in the Battle of Britain during World War II. Finally, there is the Innocent's Corner. Here rests a small urn containing bones which are said to be those of the young princes Edward V and Richard of York, murdered in the Tower of London, and the monuments of the princesses Sophia and Mary, daughters of James I, who died while still infants. Sophia is represented lying in a cradle of delicately carved alabaster, with a touching inscription: "Sophia, royal rosebud, by death torn away too soon."

Upon a bridgelike structure standing in front of the entrance to the Chapel of Henry VII is the Chapel of Henry V. Sheltered beneath this canopy—which supports an altar—is Henry's tomb, surmounted by a wooden effigy of the king. This effigy originally had a face and hands of gilded silver, but these were stolen during the Reformation. They have been replaced only in the last few years with carvings of polyester resin.

Henry's queen, Catherine of Valois, lies near her husband. Henry VII wished his beloved grandmother to lie in his chapel, and her body was disinterred during the building of the chapel with the intention of placing her there. But she in fact never occupied the place planned for her.

Over the centuries Westminster Abbey has served as a monastery, a mausoleum, a parliament, and even a mint. Beyond the church proper are the arcaded cloisters of the former monastery where, until it was dissolved in 1540, the monks went about their daily business. The adjacent chapter house, a large octagonal chamber with a single slender pillar supporting the roof, was the meeting place of the House of Commons from 1257 until the reign of Henry VIII. Its patterned tile floor dates from the thirteenth century. Near the chapter house is a small room, the Chapel of the Pyx, which takes its name from the case containing specimen coins of gold and silver which were used as standards by the Royal Mint. Parts of this low, vaulted chapel—the earliest remaining portion of the abbey built by Edward the Confessor—date back to the eleventh century.

The Norman undercroft, or crypt, now houses a museum. A vaulted space with two naves that lies at the end of the East Cloister, it was probably at one time a common room for the monks. A popular display there now is the collection of wax death masks and fully costumed funeral effigies. The practice of carrying an effigy in a funeral procession grew out of the earlier tradition of displaying the king's corpse at his funeral, which served to assure the populace that the late sovereign had died of natural causes and that his successor had come by the crown honestly. It is believed that the first such effigy was made for the funeral of Henry III, builder of the abbey.

Westminster Abbey has survived wars, revolutions, fire, and even the Protestant Reformation. The abbey is a "royal peculiar," which means that its dean is responsible only to the Crown and to God. For this reason and because of its many secular functions—as royal mausoleum, repository for the Royal Mint, and Parliament—the abbey escaped the depredations suffered by so many English monasteries after the Reformation.

Today, Westminster Abbey is the shrine of England, a place that safeguards the

Left, a procession of judges on their way from the abbey to the Houses of Parliament.

Below, Westminster Abbey and the Houses of Parliament. The Parliament buildings were built in the Neo-Gothic style by Charles Barry and Augustus Pugin between 1840 and 1867. Note the impressive bulk of Victoria Tower and, in the background, the steepled clock tower of Big Ben whose chimes are known throughout the world.

memories of a nation with a long, rich, and glorious history. But the abbey does not belong solely to the past. Just as Thorney Island is no longer an island, the abbey now sits, black and massive, a hundred yards from the Thames in the heart of metropolitan London. Across the road stand Big Ben and the Houses of Parliament. Like the British monarchy, the abbey remains a symbol of a country that

has distilled from its history one of the most tolerant and genuinely civilized societies the West has yet produced. During the coronation of a new monarch, Westminster Abbey comes most magnificently into its own. As the Archbishop of Canterbury anoints the new sovereign with consecrated oil, the ancient stones resound again with the cry of "God Save the King" or "God Save the Queen."

Temple of Horyuji

Japan

Preceding page, a panoramic view of Horyuji near Nara, Japan, one of the oldest Japanese temple complexes in existence.

Left, the central gate (Chumon) of the Temple of Horyuji.

Below left, the pagoda, seen above the covered passageway (Kairo) which encloses the temple grounds. The roof of the central gate is seen to the right, with the Golden Hall (Kondo) to the rear. The Golden Hall is aptly named, for it houses a priceless collection of seventh-century Buddhist art.

Right, two details of the Golden Hall. The elaborately carved dragons are designed to repel spirits inimical to Buddhism.

Facing page, detail showing the external bracketing of the Golden Hall and the decorations on the roof tiles.

Above, the central gate, with passageways projecting from both sides. The gate is unusual because it has two entrances.

Below, the Lecture Hall (Kodo), where the priests met to study Buddhist texts. Constructed in 990, the Lecture Hall differs in style from other parts of the temple.

Right, a thirteenth-century Shoro—a bell tower in the Eastern Precinct.

Left, two views of the interior of the Golden Hall which contains the finest examples of Buddhist art of the Asuka period (A.D. 552–645). The red-painted columns (far left) have entasis, a slight swelling at the middle, characteristic of Greek architecture and unusual in Japan. Below, the Sacred Spirit Hall (Shoryoin), a small chapel dedicated to Prince Shotoku. It is part of a building called the East Quarters (Higashimuro), originally used as lodging for the monks. Prince Shotoku reigned as prince regent from 593 to 622 and did much to spread the faith of Buddhism.

Right, a plan of Horyuji, made after A.D. 1000. Easily recognizable are the central gate, the pagoda, and the Golden Hall.

Below right, the interior of the Relic Hall (Shariden) in the Eastern Precinct.

Above, the celestial musicians above the Shaka Buddha (historic Buddha) in the Golden Hall. The musicians are descending to earth along with Buddha to welcome to paradise a devotee who has just died, in this case Prince Shotoku. Below, a statue of Kissho Ten, the goddess of happiness and good fortune. Left, the Amida Buddha, who personifies eternal life. This statue stands in the Hall of Paintings (Edono) in the Eastern Precinct. Facing page, one of the bodhisattvas beside the Buddha Sakyamuni, sculpted in 623 by Tori Busshi, the greatest artist of the period. A bodhisattva denies himself nirvana so that he can redeem others. Following page, the Western Precinct of Horyuji.

Temple of Horyuji Japan

In A.D. 710, the city of Nara was founded in Japan. It was the first city to be built specifically as the capital of that island nation. However, its pre-eminence as a political center was short-lived. In A.D. 784, the Emperor Kammu, concerned by the increasing power of the Buddhist priesthood at Nara, moved his capital to a location more convenient for sea trade, a city which eventually became the present-day Kyoto.

This abandonment turned out to be a kind of salvation for the city of Nara and the nearby temple complex of Horyuji. Time and change have passed the temple by, so that it has remained virtually un-touched by the centuries. Unlike the ancient temples at Kyoto, the shrines at Horyuji are not overshadowed by modern buildings but stand hidden and isolated in cedar and cypress woods.

Like every place of historic and artistic interest in Japan, Horyuji by day is host to an unending stream of visitors, from young girls in school uniforms to elderly women in kimonos and sandals. But at sunset the tourists disappear, and an ancient calm returns to the temple complex. Few visitors choose to stay overnight in the gracious and traditional hotels of nearby Nara. At Horyuji there is no night life in the way of theaters, bars, or clubs. But those who visit the temple at evening, wandering the serene grounds, where the only sounds are the rustle of leaves and the muffled movement of deer, can feel themselves a part of a bygone age.

Horyuji is the oldest and most venerable of the shrines at Nara, but it is by no means the largest or most immediately striking. Many visitors come only to see the Great Buddha Hall (Daibutsuden), which is the chief attraction of the Todaiji (Great Eastern Temple) complex. Founded in A.D. 738, the Todaiji complex occupies over sixty city blocks in the heart of Nara. The Great Buddha Hall, measuring over 160 feet high and 190 feet long, is reputed to be the largest wooden structure in the world; and it houses the Great Buddha (Daibutsu), one of the largest bronze statues in the world. Completed in 749, the statue is 53 feet high and weighs 550 tons.

The impressive scale of the Todaiji is a manifestation of the Japanese ambition to rival the grandeur of China during the T'ang dynasty (618–907 A.D.)—an attempt to show that the pupil had surpassed the master. The temple itself epitomizes in many ways the Buddhist building of the eighth century. It stands as the culmination of the rapid expansion of Buddhist monasteries and shrines during the seventh century, when their number rose sharply from forty-six in 624 to over five hundred in 692.

Next to the grand scale of the Todaiji, the appeal of Horyuji, a smaller and older group of buildings seven miles outside Nara, seems modest. But without Horyuji

Left, a ceiling painting in the Relic Hall showing the Buddha surrounded by a mandala.

Left, two panels from a paper door in the Golden Hall.

Below, a wooden statue in the Golden Hall depicting one of the four Celestial Kings who watch over the universe.

Far left, a Jizo bodhisattva.

Left, Yumetagai (dream changing) Kannon in the Treasure Museum at Horyuji. Yumetagai Kannon was believed to console those suffering from nightmares.

there would have been no Todaiji; without the sculpture within its walls, the Great Buddha would never have been cast. If the Todaiji epitomizes the vigor of Buddhism in Japan, the Temple of Horyuji, when it was built, stood at the crossroads of past and future. It is both a summation of Buddhist architecture through the end of the sixth century and a prediction of temples to come.

The construction of Horyuji and other temples was instrumental in establishing the Buddhist religion in Japan, which eventually supplanted Shintoism as the national religion. In comparison to Buddhism, Shintoism was a primitive collection of fatalistic superstitions without any organizing principle or theory for explaining the universe. Buddhism, on the other hand, offered a coherent and comprehensive system of cosmic and moral order, stressing man's responsibility both for his own actions and for improving the world.

Buddhist influences had filtered slowly into Japan throughout the sixth century. For instance, in 522, a gilded bronze Buddha was sent as an official gift by the emperor of the Korean state of Paikche to the

Emperor Kimmei of Japan. The Korean emperor hoped through his gift to enlist Japan as an ally in his struggle with Silla, a neighboring kingdom. Along with the statue he sent some sacred texts and a decisively worded proclamation which began: "This doctrine is amongst all doctrines the most excellent."

Buddhism also gained ground in Japan because—along with the philosophical teachings loosely allied with Confucianism—it came to be identified with the cultural achievements of the Buddhist regimes in China and Korea. In 562, the Japanese lost Mimana, their enclave on the continent, to the kingdom of Silla. This loss, in the words of one historian, "brought home to them the fact that their country was backward in everything but sheer fighting spirit." The country's leaders recognized that Japan would do well to emulate the Chinese system of centralized government. Otherwise, the divisiveness and treachery of the clans would leave their country vulnerable to attack.

In 587, the victory of the Buddhist Soga family over the Mononobe, a militant clan who were followers of Shintoism, brought

Above, the monk Gyoshin, who rebuilt the Eastern Precinct. This unusually realistic portrait, made around 750, may be the oldest extant Japanese portrait of a priest. Below, a statue of A-kei, one of the two Ni-O, or Guardian Kings, guarding the central gate. The Ni-O are sworn protectors of Buddhism. A-kei, meaning exhaling, is a symbol of goodness and light.

an end to the period of religious strife in Japan and established the pre-eminence of Buddhism. Largely responsible for the growth of the new faith was Shotoku Taishi, who became prince regent in 593. Shotoku was a man of exceptional ability and vision. He sent scholarly deputations to China and wrote learned commentaries on the sacred *sutras,* or scripture, of Buddhism. He is also believed to be the author of the so-called Constitution of the Seventeen Articles, which was issued in 604. This document—whose intent was roughly comparable to that of the Magna Carta—set out the moral and political principles which the author considered essential for national reform.

In 607, at the bidding of the Empress Suiko, Prince Shotoku undertook the construction of Horyuji. It was designed as a temple suitable for a votive Buddha, which had been commissioned in the hope that it might restore the health of Shotoku's ailing uncle, the retired emperor.

Two followers of the deity Fudo, the Immovable One. Left, Kongara Doji, symbolizing the sustaining virtue of Fudo. Below, Seitaka Doji, symbolizing his subjugating power.

One of the oldest Buddhist temples in Japan, Horyuji consists of two parts, the Western Precinct and the Eastern Precinct. The Western Precinct was the original monastery. Later, the Eastern Precinct became part of the complex, when it was made the site of a memorial to Prince Shotoku.

The architectural arrangement of the Western Precinct is an innovative departure from the Chinese designs that had previously been followed. In traditional temple plans, buildings are aligned along an axis with the central gate. The pagoda stands in front of the Golden Hall (Kondo), and the Lecture Hall (Kodo) behind it. Whatever their size, these temples always have a careful, complex symmetry. Horyuji, however, follows an asymmetric yet harmonious design which was the result of certain hierarchical problems.

When the Western Precinct of Horyuji was constructed in 607, its layout conformed to the traditional axial design. But about sixty years later, the whole complex burned to the ground, with the exception of a memorial shrine to Prince Shotoku which was set apart from the other build-

ings. It was decided to incorporate the shrine into the rebuilt temple as the new Golden Hall.

To accomplish this, the architects first had to decide how to accommodate two figures of equal stature in the Buddhist pantheon. The Shaka, or historic, Buddha was sacred to the shrine, while the Yakushi, or healing, Buddha was sacred to the monastery. Both were equally sacred to the memory of Prince Shotoku. Eventually, they were installed side by side in the Golden Hall, neither one touching upon the axis of the building. This duality set the tone for the entire compound: The pagoda and the Golden Hall are situated side by side rather than one in front of the other; the central gate (Chumon) has a pair of openings rather than one or three; and until the construction of the Lecture Hall in the tenth century, none of the elements of the temple was situated on the axis.

Symmetry is further avoided by the position of the central gate in the covered passageway (Kairo). The gate stands slightly off center, so that the passage is longer on the left side than on the right. This arrangement compensates for the

imbalance in shape and position between the pagoda and the Golden Hall. It is this careful lack of symmetry that contributes to the subtlety and sophistication of the design of Horyuji.

The pagoda stands to the left of the central gate. Traditionally, a pagoda symbolizes the burial place of the Buddha and houses a Buddha relic. The five-story pagoda at Horyuji is built on a raised stone foundation. The height of the columns in each story is less than the one below, so that the top story is exactly half the height of the ground floor. This design, which is not apparent to the casual observer, imparts a quality of lightness and grace to the building.

The Golden Hall, to the right of the central gate, is the oldest wooden building in the world and the nucleus of Horyuji. The simplicity of its layout and design makes it a classic example of the Buddhist architectural heritage adopted by Japan.

One remarkable characteristic of this building is that its pillars are shaped with the slight swelling in the middle known as entasis, which is also typical of Greek columns. It has been suggested that this device, which prevents the columns from appearing to sag inward, may have arrived from Greece by way of India and China. And interestingly enough, the stiff, inscrutable smiles of the oldest statues at Horyuji recall the archaic smile of ancient Greece.

With the addition of the Lecture Hall and the extension of the passageway in the tenth century, the Western Precinct, or Sai-in, of Horyuji took on the form it has today. It was linked to the Eastern Precinct by an avenue of white sand.

The Eastern Precinct was originally the site of a palace built by Prince Shotoku for his use when he came to meditate and study the Buddhist scriptures. This palace later burned down, and in the eighth century a small shrine, known as the Eastern Temple, or To-in, was erected by the monk Gyoshin in the prince's memory. Gyoshin played a significant role in reconciling the opposing religions of Buddhism and Shintoism. The shrine he built to Prince Shotoku contains the octagonal House of Dreams (Yumedono), supposedly based on the building used for meditation by the prince, and is perhaps the most beautiful building in the complex.

The Eastern Precinct now functions, for the most part, as a museum. It contains, among other buildings, the Hall of Paintings (Edono) and the Relic Hall (Shariden) as well as a valuable collection of art accumulated from all over Japan.

Horyuji is a repository of early Buddhist art. Its Golden Hall houses bronze sculptures dating from the sixth and seventh centuries—older than any still extant in China. Also here are the principal works of Tori Busshi, the first great sculptor of Japan. He is credited with the Yakushi and Shaka Buddhas in the Golden Hall, which were cast in 623 in memory of Prince Shotoku. In addition, the skill and variety of lacquer painting at Horyuji is unequaled among existing works of art in China or Korea.

Horyuji was first and foremost a monastery, a center of learning that helped spread the beliefs of Buddhism. Just as the medieval monasteries were havens of intellectual thought in Europe, establishments like Horyuji nurtured the flowering of Buddhist culture in Japan. The Temple of Horyuji, with its ageless serenity, thus contributed to the transformation of the life and faith of the Japanese people—a transformation as complete and dramatic as that effected by the "opening" of Japan to the West in the nineteenth century.

Above, a Shaka Buddha triad at Horyuji.

Left, detail of an attendant figure bodhisattva Seishi in the Paradise of Amida Buddha, *a mural on the west wall of the Golden Hall. In 1949, a fire, reportedly sparked by a workman's cigarette, severely damaged the painting.*

Preceding page, the Royal Square, or Maydan-i-Shah, of Isfahan, with the Mosque of the Shah in the foreground. On the right of the square stands the Mosque of Sheik Lotfollah, the private oratory of the shah.

Facing page, the dome of the mosque and the main iwan (arched half dome within a façade), flanked by two minarets. Above, one of the ornate niches in the central courtyard. Right, a portion of the eastern iwan with its polychrome ceramics. Below, the western iwan crowned by the gol-dasteh, the wooden pavilion from which the imam (prayer leader) calls the faithful to prayer.

Above, the dome of the mosque, rising above its unadorned exterior walls. It is decorated with polychrome, enameled ceramics. The "Tree of Paradise" motif, so popular in Islamic art, covers the entire surface of the massive dome. The blue band around the top of the drum supporting the dome is decorated with sayings from the Koran.

Right, the dome as seen from the northwest corner of the courtyard—partially concealed by a slender, cylindrical minaret and the main iwan.

Above right, one of the minarets which flank the main iwan. *The geometric pattern just below the balcony is a symbolic representation of the names of Allah and Ali.*

Right, a detail of the mosaic decoration, composed of small tiles, which covers the entire surface of the minaret.

Above, the western iwan *and its reflection in the pool of the central courtyard. The pool itself is used for ritual cleansing.*

Left, part of the arcade that surrounds the inner courtyard of the mosque.

Right, a typically Islamic screen of wood and brick that fills one of the arches of the arcade surrounding the inner courtyard. Aside from its decorativeness, the screen fulfills the practical function of filtering and softening the harsh desert light before it enters the mosque.

Below, one of the colonnaded rooms adjacent to the prayer hall, with its octagonal columns supporting massive, tiled vaults. Through the arched doorway can be seen the mihrab—*the niche that indicates to the faithful the direction of Mecca, toward which they must face to pray.*

Left, the underside of the dome of the Mosque of the Shah. The dome is lit by eight windows in the supporting drum.

Below left, the interior of the eastern iwan, whose geometry is based on a ten-sided figure.

Below, an example of the complex geometry of the domes and iwans.

Facing page, examples of the styles of ceramics in the mosque: flowers, animals, and thuluth (phrases and sayings).

Following page, the inner courtyard of the mosque, an architectural realization of the following saying from the Koran: "Those who fear the Lord will in Paradise have a place surrounded by splendid arcades from which other arches will rise, and they will see their reflections in clear waters." (Chapter XXXIX)

Mosque of the Shah

Isfahan

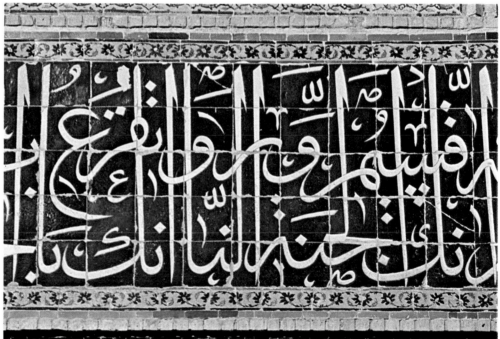

Mosque of the Shah Isfahan

The Mosque of the Shah, or Masjid-i-Shah, represents the greatest triumph of Shah Abbas I (Abbas the Great) who ruled Persia from 1587 to 1628. A prolific builder and enlightened ruler, he envisioned the mosque both as an assertion of his temporal power and as a monument to Shiism, the newly established religion of the kingdom. As self-proclaimed leader of the sect, he needed an appropriately magnificent mosque that would reflect his sovereignty. Thus, the Mosque of the Shah—an awesome sanctuary that rises like a blue mirage out of the city of Isfahan.

Below, a seventeenth-century miniature showing the Royal Square as it appeared when Isfahan was the capital of the Safavid kingdom. The square is actually a huge rectangle whose longest side measures 1,500 feet. The royal palace, the bazaar, and the two mosques all open out onto the square.

In the spring of 1598, Abbas left the royal capital of Qazvin and established Isfahan as the capital of his kingdom. A large and flowering oasis lying between the mountains of a high plateau in central Iran, the city became the center of a Persian cultural and artistic renaissance during Abbas' reign.

This renaissance flourished in an era of political stability in Persia. At the beginning of the sixteenth century, Shah Ismail I (1499–1524), the great-grandfather of Abbas I, had united Persia politically, culturally, and religiously under Safavid rule. The Safavid dynasty began with Ismail's expulsion of Mongolian and Turkish invaders and continued until 1722, when Persia was overrun by the Afghans. During this period, Isfahan rose in prominence, not only as the economic and artistic capital of Persia but also as the center for the practice of Shiism. This branch of Islam holds Ali—the cousin and son-in-law of Mohammed—and his descendants to be the only true spiritual leaders of the Moslem faith.

Abbas I was indisputably the greatest of the Safavid monarchs. According to a contemporary report, he was "bright-witted, martial, mercurial, strong, skillful, healthy, resolute, with a good memory, and sagacious in business." Abbas encouraged visitors, especially Christians, and hundreds of Europeans came to the

Persian capital during his reign. Many of them returned to their homelands with inspired accounts of the city's splendors and curiosities.

Abbas was also exceedingly superstitious and rarely made state decisions without first conferring with his astrologers. Apparently, he was insanely cautious, even by the standards of his day, and had his own sons either killed or mutilated—actions he is said to have later regretted bitterly. Yet, Abbas is quoted as saying that he "would have killed a hundred children in order to reign alone a single day."

Abbas transformed the already thriving commercial center of Isfahan into a city of impressive beauty and architectural interest. Throughout his reign, he undertook lavish construction—often at a feverish and, according to his architects, destructive pace—to make Isfahan into a capital befitting a shah. He also encouraged every form of art, from carpet weaving to metalworking, and created a city that dazzled even European visitors accustomed to the splendors of Versailles.

Isfahan is not famous solely for Abbas' Mosque of the Shah but also for his buildings that surround the city's Royal Square, or Maydan-i-Shah. The Royal Square, the hub of the city during Abbas' reign, was used for festivals, games (mainly polo), and markets. On its west side Abbas built

Left, Mohammed and his family in a seventeenth-century miniature. The Islamic religion theoretically forbids pictorial representations of Allah, but there are numerous illustrated biographies of Mohammed.

Below, a Persian miniature showing the foothills between Persia and Tibet. At its height, Islam stretched from the Atlantic to the Pacific oceans and far north into Europe.

government offices and a luxurious palace called the Ali Quapu, and on the east was the Mosque of Sheik Lotfollah, the shah's private chapel.

The north side of the square gradually evolved into an immense bazaar, where peddlers and stall owners offered a vast assortment of foreign and domestic wares. Here, travelers from Europe and China mingled with Middle Easterners of all nationalities in the lively cosmopolitan atmosphere of the richest city in the Persian

empire. During the reign of Abbas I, Isfahan became a mecca both for traders bringing goods from the West and East and for travelers eager to see the artistic wonders of Persia.

All of the shah's buildings on the Royal Square were connected by a wall that was inset with arched niches. Behind this wall, Abbas planted trees and lush gardens surrounded by pools and canals. He also laid out a broad ceremonial avenue, the Avenue of the Four Gardens, or Chahar Bagh,

that leads up to the complex. For the city, the shah designed a more sophisticated system of roads as well as more waterways. And over the Zayandeh River he built a bridge nearly a thousand feet long with thirty-three arches.

The Mosque of the Shah, situated on the southern side of the square opposite the Royal Bazaar, was begun in 1612 and completed in 1638, almost a decade after Abbas' death. With its surrounding court-

Left, a corner of the Royal Square, dominated by the great mosque and by the tribune above the entrance to the palace of Abbas I. The square is surrounded by two splendidly ornamented arcades, one above the other.

Left, the entrance to the Mosque of the Shah. The city of Isfahan reached its peak during the reign of Abbas I, with more than 600,000 inhabitants, but in the second half of the eighteenth century, the capital of the empire was moved first to Shiraz and then to Tehran.

yards and gardens and its harmonious proportions, the mosque represents the culmination of religious building under the Safavids. Abbas based his design on the Timurid Mosque of Gauhar Shad in Mashhad, built three hundred years earlier. While decidedly inferior to the Timurid Mosque in its details, the Mosque of the Shah is considerably more impressive—as Abbas intended it to be.

Since the *mihrab* (niche) in the prayer wall of a mosque must face toward Mecca, Abbas' perfectly symmetrical mosque is situated assymetrically in relation to the *maydan* (square). As a result, the main *iwan* (arched half dome within a façade) at the entrance to the mosque's courtyard is at a forty-five degree angle to the *iwan* opening onto the square. Thus, the area between the portals is in the shape of a triangle with two equal sides. If such an unusually shaped space had been part of either the square or mosque, it would have ruined their symmetry.

To preserve symmetry, the doorways of the mosque were placed on the sides of the *iwan* facing the central court rather than in the center. These portals, instead of being

Right, a miniature from a manuscript by Nizami, a Persian poet of the twelfth century, showing a king as he chances upon a young woman bather.

connected directly to the *maydan*, are reached through two corridors of unequal length issuing from a pair of circular vestibules. These, in turn, join a central, larger vestibule that leads out to the *maydan*. Since visitors entering from the *maydan* cannot pass down both corridors at the same time, they are unaware of the lack of symmetry.

Though similar in function, mosques of different countries vary in basic design. The typical Arab mosque is a large colonnaded hall, while the usual Turkish de-

sign, derived from Byzantine churches, uses a massive dome with supporting half domes. Persian mosques are distinguished not only by an interior domed space but also by a large central courtyard with four porticoed façades, each with a central *iwan* leading to a hall. The courtyard gives Persian mosques the shape of a hollow-centered cross, the huge central space being domed only by the sky.

Abbas departed slightly from the traditional Persian mosque design in his Mosque of Sheik Lotfollah but kept to the classical arrangement in the Mosque of the Shah. In the middle of his central courtyard, Abbas built a large ablution pool in which the surrounding *iwans* and arcades are reflected. As one circles the courtyard, the dome and minarets form a compelling and vigorous design. At one point, the dome—standing one hundred sixty feet above the ground—rises commandingly above the court, dominating all perspectives. At another vantage point, the *iwan* cuts the curve of the dome, while both are complemented vertically by the minarets. These varying perspectives are a spectacular preparation for the beauty of the interior.

Throughout his reign, Abbas made extensive use of the *haft-rangi*, or seven-color tile. As opposed to the true mosaic tile work of the Timurid and early Safavid periods, where each single-hued tile is individually cut to fit into an intricate design, *haft-rangi* tiles are mainly square. Though the brilliance of the former method was sacrificed, *haft-rangi* tiles made it possible to cover vast surfaces more quickly and with less expense. Fortunately, the use of *haft-rangi* tile at the Mosque of the Shah is not altogether regrettable. The central court of the mosque is so spectacular in its own right that true mosaics might have seemed overpowering and excessive.

While the color of the ceramics is perhaps most immediately striking, equally important are the arabesques the tiles portray. These traditional designs mainly represent fertility and abundance. At the apex of the dome, a golden sun radiates warmth and life through expanding tendrils of vibrant foliage. There is scarcely a surface that is not crowded with intricate floral designs. Even the openings in the grilles around the drum of the dome are in the form of flowing vines. Throughout the mosque, the abstract imagery of the tile work reflects the Moslem vision of heaven as a place of flowing streams and abundant gardens.

The Mosque of the Shah, both in its plan and its individual parts, has no specific religious symbolism. Unlike Western churches, there are no altars, no privileged places, no special ceremonies, and no sacred objects. The sole function of the *mihrab*, for example, is to direct worshipers toward Mecca. Further, the spiritual democracy of Islam is manifest in the unobstructed ground plan of the mosque, which reflected the Moslem belief that god hears all prayers equally.

To a degree, Shah Abbas' main concern in building the mosque was not so much for the spiritual welfare of his subjects as for his own personal ambitions. He was adamant that his mosque should overshadow all neighboring mosques and that construction should be completed as rapidly as possible. In fact, he actually ordered that construction begin on the walls before the foundations had set. Only at the insistence of his architects was he finally persuaded to withdraw this command.

The mosque suffered structurally as a result of the shah's obsession with speed. Like most large buildings on the Iranian plateau, the mosque was made primarily of brick, which is well suited to an area that frequently experiences earthquakes. But because the mosque's foundation was laid with such uncertain workmanship, frequent repairs were necessary.

However, the overall effect of the mosque compensates for any defects in detail. The restrained geometric plan of the mosque is complemented by the sheer exuberance and sensual appeal of its brilliantly colored tiles. Reigning over the green oasis of Isfahan and guarded by its sentinel-like minarets, the Mosque of the Shah attests to the power of its creator and his once-powerful empire.

Below, an eighteenth-century engraving of the Mosque of the Shah, which depicts two of the iwans. *These vaulted spaces set within the façade are typical of both Islamic and Persian architecture.*

Chartres Cathedral

France

Preceding page, view of the south side of Chartres Cathedral. The celebrated Gothic church stands on a slight rise and dominates its surroundings in the Beauce region of France. Left, the vieux clocher (old bell tower) on the southwest corner of the cathedral. Above, the intersecting flying buttresses of the choir and transept. The cycle of statues that adorns the cathedral, especially its doorways, is one of the most extensive—and the most deservedly famous—in all of French art. The tympanum (below) of the south transept depicts the stories of Saint Martin and Saint Nicholas. Facing page, above, the south transept of Chartres with typical thirteenth-century linear form. Below, left and right, the flying buttresses around the east end of the cathedral, rebuilt in the fourteenth century.

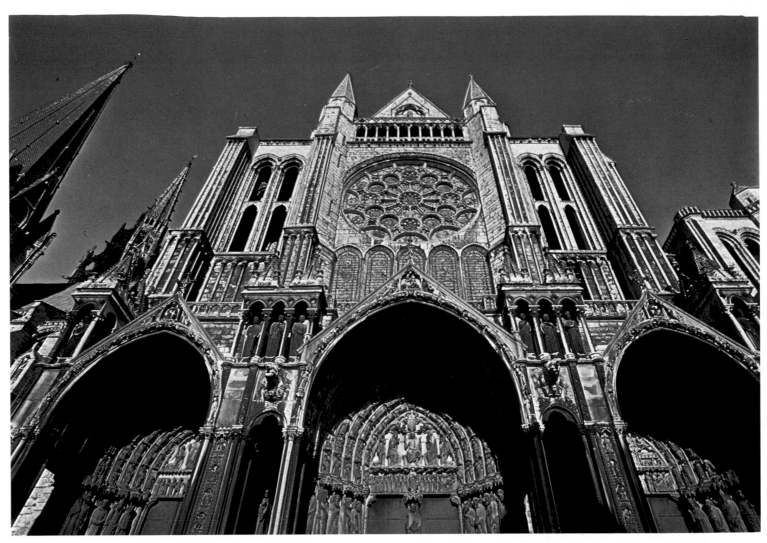

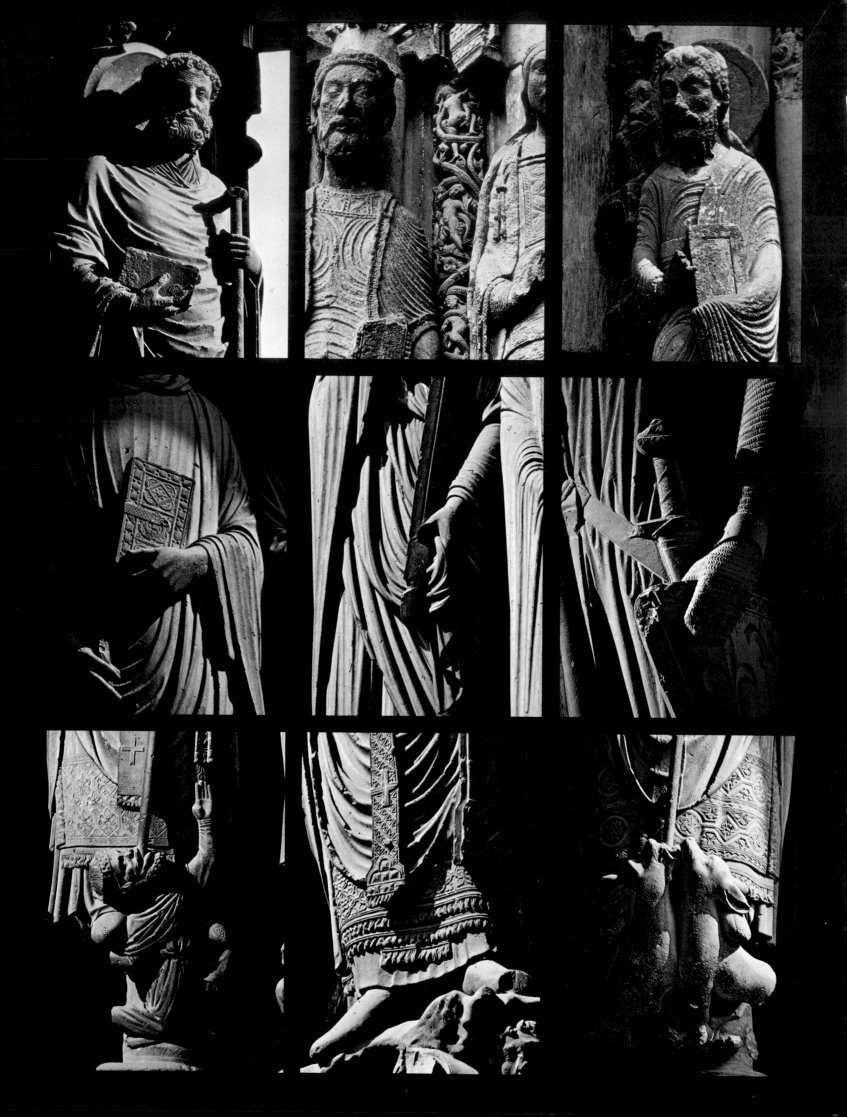

The exterior of Chartres is covered with sculpted figures (facing page), which are ancestors, forerunners, or Apostles of Christ. Each figure is identified by its particular attribute. Top row, left, Avit, Abbot of Micy (south porch); center and right, two kings of Juda (west façade). Middle row, left, Saint John, holding his gospel and a fragment of a palm (south porch); center, Saint Thomas the Apostle, holding the sword of his martyrdom (south porch); right, Saint George, dressed in chain mail with a sword and shield signifying his role as a military tribune in Diocletian's bodyguard (south porch). Bottom row, left, Saint Ambrose, Bishop of Milan, forcing the end of his crozier into the mouth of Maximus who made himself emperor in opposition to Valentinian (south porch); center, Saint Leo, standing on a pedestal of three heads (south porch); right, Saint Martin, Bishop of Tours, said to have had a miraculous power over animals. Here he is shown with two dogs at his feet. As time evolved, the geometric carving of the twelfth century (top row, middle and right) gave way to the more naturalistic forms of the thirteenth century (top row, left).

Above, a portion of the Incarnation Portal on the west façade. Reading from left to right, these pairs of twelfth-century figures portray the Annunciation, Visitation, and the Virgin lying in childbirth. Right, twelfth-century figures representing the ancestors of Christ on the west façade.

The interior of Chartres, one of the most harmonious to be found anywhere in France, has become a standard by which all Gothic architecture is judged. Above, detail of the four-part vaulting which covers the nave of the cathedral. Left, a view of the lofty, three-story elevation in the nave. The ambulatory (below) winds around the eastern end of the church. Facing page, view of the interior looking west toward the main entrance.

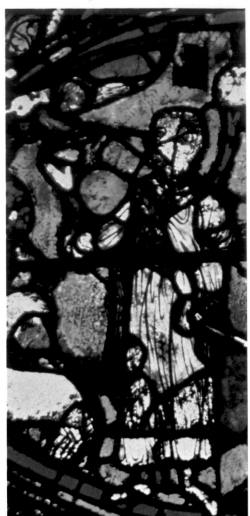

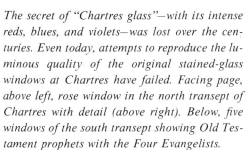

The secret of "Chartres glass"—with its intense reds, blues, and violets—was lost over the centuries. Even today, attempts to reproduce the luminous quality of the original stained-glass windows at Chartres have failed. Facing page, above left, rose window in the north transept of Chartres with detail (above right). Below, five windows of the south transept showing Old Testament prophets with the Four Evangelists.

Right, the Crucifixion as seen on the twelfth-century Passion window on the west façade. Above, the history of Saint James. Above center, the story of Saint Lubin, patron saint of wine. The window was donated by the wine-makers guild. Above right, the story of Christ.

Following page, southeast view of Chartres at sunset.

Chartres Cathedral France

Chartres Cathedral can be seen towering protectively over the wheat fields on the plain of Beauce long before the picturesque city which surrounds it comes into view. From a distance, the church's steeple and bell tower, often described as "the fingers of God," seem to rise ethereally toward heaven. In an age that is becoming increasingly secular, Chartres Cathedral offers a rare insight into the medieval mind's unquestioning dedication to the glory of God and almost religious pride in craftsmanship.

of Christ. Evidence suggests that a Christian building occupied the site even at the time of the Roman Empire. A church has remained at Chartres throughout the centuries in spite of several fires that threatened the cathedral between 700 and 1000 A.D.

Throughout its history, the greatest pride of Chartres Cathedral has been what was believed to be a piece of the Virgin's tunic. Understandably, the citizens of Chartres and their bishop, Fulbert de Chartres, felt a tremendous sense of loss when their cathedral was devastated by another fire on July 10, 1194, leaving only parts of the façade, the crypt, and the bases of the western towers. But when a cleric discovered the sacred relic of the Virgin's cloak, unharmed among the smoking ruins, the townspeople turned mourning into jubilation and immediately began construction on a new, even grander cathedral.

This enthusiasm was at least partially re-

sponsible for the comparatively short time in which most of Chartres Cathedral was rebuilt. In just twenty-seven years, the remnants of Bishop Fulbert's original church were integrated into a new cathedral that exhibited a remarkable harmony of style. The construction of Chartres seems almost miraculously short when compared to other medieval cathedrals, which normally took decades, even centuries, to complete; wars, famine, plague, and insufficient funds invariably intervened and slowed construction.

Nevertheless, the medieval cathedrals always remained at the heart of city life. They not only answered the spiritual needs of the populace but also served a variety of secular functions, often doubling as a community center, market, hospital, or refuge. Many medieval townspeople were also economically dependent on the church since it owned considerable tracts of land in the outlying areas and held annual trade fairs that brought com-

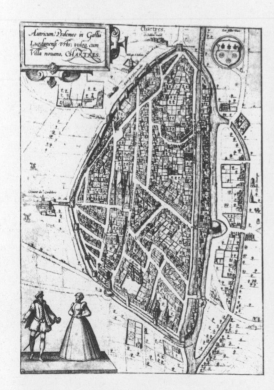

The religious history of the town of Chartres and its cathedral dates back to early Gallic times when the Druids worshiped a virgin mother in the village's grottoes. Because the virgin idol had striking similarities with her Christian counterpart, the cult and the Druid sanctuary were eventually adopted by the followers

Far left, map depicting Chartres as it appeared in the fifteenth century.

Left, a nineteenth-century view of Chartres showing the "vieux clocher" and the newer, more flamboyant tower which was added in the sixteenth century.

merce to the city. As the wealthiest local institution and the greatest patron of the arts, cathedrals promised work to generations of masons, carpenters, smiths, glaziers, and common laborers. It is even recorded that, on one occasion, nobility and common folk alike strapped themselves to carts and hauled masonry and other building materials to the construction site.

There were no architects in medieval

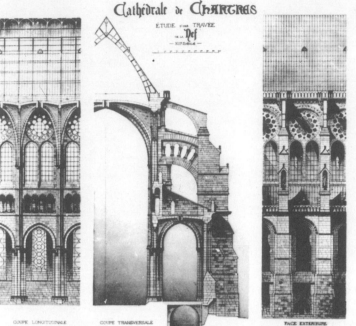

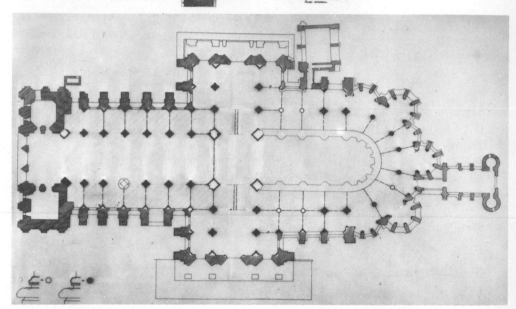

Far left, reconstruction of a project for the façade of 1194.

Left, interior elevation, section, and exterior elevation of the nave.

Below, a plan of the cathedral.

times. Instead, master masons directed and supervised all construction. They were trained during a seven-year apprenticeship and committed all knowledge to memory. For a time, the "secrets of the master mason" were closely guarded against dissemination. In fact, it is recorded that Bishop Conrad of Utrecht was murdered by his master mason in 1099 because the bishop had obtained "the secret." This rather extreme case illustrates the strength of the conviction that construction and design methods should be kept within the guilds. Plans for early Gothic cathedrals were drawn out on plasterboard, which was recoated as soon as they were no longer needed. And even these drawings were merely schematic, with no precise indications of measure-

ments or techniques of construction.

Quite unlike today's scientific methods, Gothic cathedrals developed by trial and error. Master masons actively experimented with possible solutions to construction problems. If the solutions worked, they were used again, but if they didn't, the techniques—and the architectural mutations they created—would eventually disappear.

One of the most dramatic examples of this experimental technique is the evolution of the flying buttress, a development that is integral both to the beauty and to the structural purity of Chartres. In an attempt to develop a fireproof ceiling that would replace the wooden ceilings of earlier churches, master masons turned to heavy stone vaults. But because of their

weight, the vaults had to be supported by walls as much as twelve to sixteen feet thick, in which windows could be little more than holes. During the twelfth century, builders invented vaults that channeled the pressure of their weight into the corners of the bay. Thus, buttressing was needed only at the four corners of a vault. This development allowed the builders to rotate the mass of the walls—now buttresses—ninety degrees so that they were perpendicular to the main axis of the church.

Where there once had to be heavy masonry, there was now the opportunity for relatively large open spaces, which glaziers filled with windows of unprecedented size and beauty. To support the nave vaults in the center of the church, masons erected arches, or flying buttresses, on the exterior of the high walls and connected them above the side aisles with the major exterior buttresses.

At Chartres, the flying buttresses underwent further modifications and refinements. When Chartres was being built in the early thirteenth century, masons used tremendously heavy buttresses, still seen along the sides of the church, to support the 122-foot vaults. But in 1316, the Expertise of Chartres, a group of masons brought in to make structural adjustments, encouraged the use of lighter, more slender fliers. These elegant supports, found at the back of the cathedral, represent the full maturity of the aesthetic and structural possibilities of the flying buttress.

The interior of Chartres Cathedral is composed of a multiplication of bays—modular units covered by four-part vaults. The side aisles are a single line of these modules, while the nave is a double-width row emphasizing the central axis that leads to the altar. Massive columns separate each bay, forming strong vertical lines, while horizontal moldings divide the elevation into three stories. The result is a complex but integrated pattern of intersecting lines, further emphasized by alternating solids and voids, highlights and shadows.

The only departure from this basic scheme is in the ambulatory turning around the apse at the eastern end where the bays abandon their standard form and become irregular trapezoids. Radiating off each of these bays were small chapels, housing relics of medieval saints. This practical arrangement allowed pilgrims to move through the church and visit the shrines of the saints without disturbing services held at the main altar.

In a sense, medieval life was thought to be one long pilgrimage from this life to the next. Since the ultimate pilgrimage to the Holy Land was not only risky but also expensive, many pilgrims elected to journey through Western Europe, visiting the churches of the holy saints. Pilgrims who had traveled long distances to reach Chartres would symbolically complete their pilgrimage, often on their knees, by following the lines of a labyrinth—a huge, circular diagram—set in the pavement of the nave.

Besides being an architectural masterpiece, Chartres is embellished with some of the most distinguished and best preserved medieval sculpture in all of Europe. Because literacy in the Middle Ages was generally the privilege of the clergy, religious sculpture became the "poor man's Bible," relating the stories of saints and holy events.

The west façade, or Royal Portal, has three doors around which the story of Christ is depicted. The entire front of the church is lined with twenty-four Old Testament figures (four are now missing) who heralded Christ's coming. In the tympana—the sculpted areas above the doors—New Testament themes are shown.

Left, the choir screen which separates the ambulatory from the chancel. Above, four panels from a twelfth-century window on the west façade depicting the life of Christ. Top, nineteenth-century engraving of the Royal Portal.

On the right is the Incarnation, in the center is the Second Coming of Christ, and on the left is the Ascension of the Savior. These three sculpted scenes are connected by a horizontal band of sculpture that depicts the story of the Virgin. The logical integration of the sculpture into the overall architectural plan of the cathedral provided the illiterate pilgrims with a visual review of their Christian heritage. At the same time, these traditional Biblical stories, preserved in stone, served to reaffirm orthodox Christian belief against various low-lying heresies, the most persistent of which had to do with the duality of Christ and the miracle of the Immaculate Conception.

Chartres was the first cathedral to decorate its lesser entrances in a major way. The two transept porches repeat the three-portal sculpture arrangement used on the Royal Portal and even continue the themes depicted there. That is, the south porch shows the Last Judgment, while the north is dedicated to the Virgin's life. This sculpture, executed in the thirteenth century, is quite lifelike, especially when compared to Bishop Fulbert's stiff, geometric statuary in the front of the church which survived the fire of 1194.

The stained glass at Chartres is as awesome as the sculpture. Today, its almost four thousand figures represent a nearly complete evolution of medieval glazing styles, ranging from the somewhat abstract forms of the twelfth century on the west façade to the more free-flowing thirteenth-century style decorating the rest of the church.

Glassmaking in the Middle Ages was so highly regarded that glass fragments were often referred to as gems, a reflection of the pre-Christian belief that glass is brought to life by the sun's rays. Thus, only the most cherished saints and Biblical events were portrayed, to the near total exclusion of demonic figures and beasts. These tapestries of glass, like the sculptures outside the cathedral, were "read" by the illiterate.

The luminous beauty of the stained glass at Chartres is best seen in relation to the life and movement of the sun. The gaze of a visitor entering the cathedral just after sunrise is first drawn to the east windows, especially those in the clerestory. They alone are fully illuminated, while the other windows remain in shadow. As the sun rises in the sky, the east windows begin to lose their brilliance to those of the southern flank of the church, which by midday are fully aglow. Late in the afternoon, the blues in the west windows, by far the most intense in the cathedral, are emblazoned. When the sky reddens at sunset, the blue is muted and the ruby-colored glass asserts itself. In a sense, the stained glass at Chartres actively—and symbolically—links the cathedral with the heavens above.

Chartres Cathedral was not intended to be merely another Christian building on earth. It aspired to reflect the transcendental perfection of the next world. The cosmos was seen as the ultimate work of architecture with God its divine architect; Chartres was envisioned as an architectural embodiment of this divine relationship. The church was built to face east because the sun rises in the east and Christ is the light of the world. The western portals were not merely doors but also symbols of the passage from this world into the next. And the stained-glass windows were analogous to the Immaculate Conception because light could penetrate them without breaking the glass—just as Mary was conceived without original sin.

Above, a nineteenth-century engraving of the countryside around Chartres with the graceful spires of the cathedral outlined against the sky.

So thoroughly accepted were these symbolic interpretations of the various parts of cathedrals that the thirteenth century produced numerous reference volumes. One such work, the *Rationale Divinorum Officiorum,* written around 1286 by Guillaume Durand, systematically explores the significance of the church and its parts. Durand explains that the nave of the church represents the body of Christ with the transepts as His arms and the rounded eastern chancel as His head. The four walls of the building are the Four Evangelists—Matthew, Mark, Luke, and John—and their height is said to represent courage, their length fortitude, and their breadth charity. The piers which support the church are perceived as bishops who support their congregations, and the pavement signifies humility.

Written documents of the Middle Ages are generally ambiguous and often incomplete. Yet, in the great cathedrals, particularly at Chartres, we have a record not only of medieval technical advances but also of the evolution of aesthetic sensibilities. Perhaps more important, Chartres provides the modern world with a visible testimony to an age of complete religious faith and dedication.

Cathedral
of Mexico City

Mexico

Preceding page, the Cathedral of Mexico City (left) and the Sagrario Metropolitano, the adjacent parish church which houses the Holy Sacrament (right). The two buildings dominate the southern end of the Zócalo, Mexico City's ancient town square, which was once the center of Aztec civilization.

Above, the façade of the Sagrario. Left, southeast view of the cathedral and the Sagrario.

The cathedral (above right), seen from the southwest. Right, the contrastingly smooth walls that flank the ornate stone entrance to the Sagrario. Far right, a stone cross in the forecourt of the cathedral. Mounted on a plumed serpent (symbol of the Aztec god-king Quetzalcoatl), the cross represents the triumph of Christianity over paganism.

Facing page, the ornate façade of the Sagrario Metropolitano. The carving, all in volcanic rock (tezontle), is one of the finest examples of the Churrigueresque style in all of Mexico.

The huge paneled doors of the cathedral (above and right) are a marked contrast to the intricate curved design of the Sagrario's doors.

The classically "correct" fluted Roman Doric columns of the cathedral (right and above left) support a vaulting system that is Gothic in conception, while the domes of the aisles echo usages of the early Renaissance. Left, the richly ornate Altar of Pardon in the central nave. Oil paintings, including the Virgin of the Pardon by Simon Pereyns, are set in a screen decorated with hundreds of gilded wood figures. The decoration is continued in the gold balconies of the choir, which are mounted on the piers.

The eighteenth-century Altar of Kings (above) in the apse of the cathedral was created by Geronimo Balbás. A masterpiece of the Churrigueresque, it holds two paintings by the famous Mexican artist Juan Rodríguez Juárez.

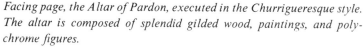

Facing page, the Altar of Pardon, executed in the Churrigueresque style. The altar is composed of splendid gilded wood, paintings, and polychrome figures.

Above, detail of the Altar of Pardon. The Chapel of the Archangels (above right) shows the entire hierarchy of the angelic host. Right, the dark-skinned Christ of the Poison. According to legend, a worshiper who had been poisoned by a rival kissed the feet of the statue, which absorbed the poison and turned black.

Following page, view of the massive cathedral and its delicate companion, the Sagrario.

Cathedral of Mexico City

The early Spanish explorers landing on the shores of the New World must have thought that they had arrived in paradise. A sea of pure, clear emerald lapped against crescent beaches of white sand bordered by luxuriant vegetation. Everything seemed ripe and abundant—and theirs for the taking. The most enticing sight of all was undoubtedly the jewelry worn by the natives who came to meet them. Shining with the unmistakable gleam of gold, it gave credence to the legend of El Dorado, the golden kingdom.

No sooner had the West Indies been subdued by Spain at the end of the fif-teenth century than rumors began to spread of the fabulous wealth of the American mainland. Hernando Cortes, a Spanish émigré working as a rancher in the Indies, was inflamed by these rumors of gold. He eventually persuaded Diego Velásquez, the governor of Cuba, to permit him to lead an expedition into Mexico. Fearing Cortes' power, the governor quickly reconsidered his approval and sent troops to arrest Cortes. Undaunted, Cortes defeated the governor's army and then won them over to his cause. Velásquez later retaliated by sending an emissary to Spain in an attempt to undermine Cortes, who, in turn, sent his own delegation, which ultimately secured the favor of the Spanish throne.

In the spring of 1519, Cortes finally got his expedition underway. Ironically, when Cortes landed in Mexico, the Aztecs welcomed him as a god. Five hundred years earlier, their legendary god-king Quetzalcoatl, banished by an enemy, had pledged to return by sea to lead his people once again. Hearing of the arrival of ships bearing bearded, white-skinned strangers, Montezuma, the Aztec emperor, sent lavish gifts of gold to the presumed god, promising to turn over the kingdom when he died. When the Spaniards continued their advance on the capital at Tenochtitlán, Montezuma made hasty preparations to relinquish his throne. Unable to believe that the empire had actually surrendered without a fight, Cortes took Montezuma prisoner. When their ruler died in Spanish custody, the Aztecs finally realized that Cortes and his men were neither gods nor well intentioned. They immediately turned on the Spaniards and routed them in a bloody battle.

Banding together with the many rival nations of the Aztecs (his Indian allies numbered over 75,000), Cortes mounted a final attack on Tenochtitlán. Guatemotzin, the nephew of Montezuma, led the Aztecs, but they could not repulse the allied forces and their Spanish cannons. Having destroyed the glorious Aztec capital, Cortes founded a new capital—Mexico City—in its place. Thousands of Indians were killed in the conquest, but far more were later to die in the gold and silver

Left, a pictorial catalogue of the tribute exacted by the Aztecs from their subjects every eighty days. This drawing shows the Indian towns on the left and on the right the payments levied. Common tributes were birds, animal skins, costumes, and food.

Above, a print depicting a group of Aztec warriors in a last desperate stand against Cortes and his band of Indian allies. The Aztecs are barricading themselves in a temple in Tenochtitlán, while Cortes' allies rally under the flag.

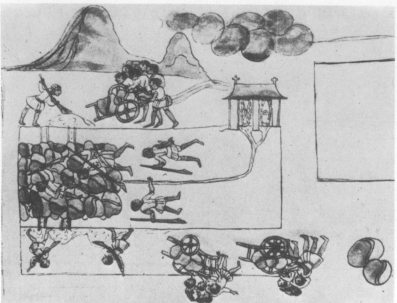

The Spanish conquistadors erected their own capital city on the site of Tenochtitlán. Far left, Mexico City as it appeared in 1524, five years after the conquest of the Aztec empire.

Left, a group of Indians working on the cathedral. Below, a drawing of the cathedral dating from the mid-sixteenth century.

mines which enriched the Spanish royal treasury.

Though plunder was highly valued by the conquerors, their professed mission was to bring the true faith of Catholicism to the Aztec nation. So the Spanish galleons that sailed home loaded with gold and silver returned to Mexico with zealous missionaries. The Franciscans arrived in 1524, the Dominicans in 1526, and the Augustinians in 1533, followed some years later by the Jesuits.

The local population obligingly converted, accepting the god of the conquerors as a victorious god. There was ample room in their polytheistic pantheon for the Catholic deity and saints. Besides, certain rites were common to Catholicism and the Aztec religion, including fasting, penance, and the use of incense and sacred ointments. The religious ceremonies of the medieval church—the music, processions, and elaborate clerical vestments—also appealed to the Aztec taste. Finally, the doctrine of the suffering and death of Christ had its parallels with the Aztec rite of human sacrifice, blood rituals in which as many as ten to twenty thousand captive warriors were put to death. These similarities facilitated the conversion, and Mexico soon became wholly and vehemently Catholic.

As Spanish dominance in Mexico grew, so did the need for new buildings to serve the conquerors. Under local influence, de-

signs imported from Spain eventually evolved into a hybrid architectural style. The great town square (Zócalo) of Mexico City was the site of much of the early construction. At the foot of the pyramids of the ancient Aztec gods, the square had been the center of Aztec society, complete with schools, hostels, ceremonial ball courts, and vast markets. It had also functioned as the seat of government, the palace of Montezuma.

The Spaniards retained the civic role of this ancient town square even as they ordered the vanquished Aztecs to destroy their old temples. On the foundations of Montezuma's palace, Cortes built his own Palacio Nacional, a splendid building in the then current Spanish Plateresque style, which takes its name from the Spanish word *platero* (silversmith). The delicate ornamentation of this style is reminiscent of decorative Spanish silver work.

In 1532, the square also became the

center of Mexican Catholicism with the completion of a small wooden church designed by the Spanish architect Martin de Sepúlveda. Called the Iglesia Mayor (principal church), it stood near the site of the pyramids of the Aztec rain and sun gods, Tlaloc and Huitzilopochtli, and even included some of their masonry in its foundations.

Shortly after this modest church was finished, Philip II of Spain decided that Mexico City, as an outpost of the Spanish Empire, ought to have a grander and more dignified house of worship. Accordingly, in a decree of October 8, 1536, he ordered a cathedral to be built on the site of the church. Despite this royal directive, no action was taken, and the decree had to be reiterated in 1544, 1551, and 1552. Finally, the question of payment was resolved, and plans were drawn up following the design of the cathedral at Seville. The plans were reconsidered when it was decided that Seville set an excessively ornate example. A new decree of May 4, 1569, established the church at Salamanca as a model, and the first stone was laid in 1573. Soon after construction began, however, these plans too were rejected in favor of a design in the Renaissance manner by the royal master of architecture, Alonso Pérez de Castanada. This irksome pattern of indecision and constant revision plagued the cathedral throughout the lengthy period of its construction.

Left, drawing by Pedro Ramirez for the catafalque in honor of Philip IV (1666).

Right, the project for the façade presented in 1778 by Geronimo Balbás.

Numerous architects contributed to the design of the cathedral over the course of nearly three centuries. Far right, the floor plan of the cathedral in a drawing by Juan Gómez de Mora.

Right, a steel engraving made around 1860 of the Plaza Mayor, with the cathedral in the background.

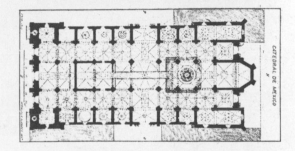

Because Mexico City was the most important settlement in New Spain, its cathedral was to be the grandest church in the entire country. As architectural fashions changed in Europe, so did the design of the cathedral. Even though Spanish architects traveled to Mexico to implement their plans and supervise construction, persistent local influence had an unmistakable effect. Eventually, the cathedral evolved into a building which, though of European inspiration, was not entirely European in form or spirit.

Construction progressed slowly. When Philip II, who had commissioned this monument to his imperial power, died in 1598, the cathedral was far from finished. In 1615, with the walls still at only half their planned height, Philip III sent yet another new design by his architect Juan Gómez de Mora. By this time, construction was too far advanced for any major structural changes; de Mora's ideas are

reflected only in the vaulting and some of the decorations of the church.

For two hundred years, construction proceeded, always modified by the latest developments in Europe. The result is a somewhat disjointed combination of Classic conception and Baroque execution. An additional complication is introduced by the reliance throughout on Gothic vaulting techniques. This blend, further interpreted and altered by the cathedral's Indian builders, yields an intriguing, if stylistically discordant, structure.

Between 1635 and 1640, five chapels were completed, seven vaults of the nave were erected, and an altar and temporary choir were installed. In 1656, the first cathedral in Mexico was finally consecrated. Celebrations lasted ten days, complete with feasts, parades, and fireworks. The interior of the cathedral, however, was not finished until 1667, whereupon the viceroy ordered a new dedication with no less

pomp than the original. The exterior, however, remained incomplete until 1813. The cathedral as it exists today is the work of no fewer than twelve architects, and its construction spanned the reigns of twelve kings as well as the tenure of fifty-seven viceroys and twenty-four bishops.

The interior plan of the cathedral is a huge rectangle 387 feet in length and 177 feet in width. The central nave is flanked on each side by an aisle and a row of small chapels. This arrangement creates a progression from the low chapels to the higher side aisles up to the towering 203-foot height of the nave. Barrel vaults overlaid with tracery create a Gothic feeling in the nave, while the side aisles and chapels are crowned by shallow domes in the Renaissance style. The twenty interior piers are of a Roman Doric order, but the fluting around the overhead arches of the nave is a distinctly Gothic touch.

Above, Ferdinand VII. During his reign, Spain—weakened by the Napoleonic Wars—lost its South American colonies.

Above right, a fresco by the native Mexican muralist Juan O'Gorman, whose work is often described as being antiecclesiastical and antifascist.

Right, the cathedral and square from an early nineteenth-century engraving by Alexander von Humboldt.

The stern quality of the architectural elements is offset by the wealth of interior sculpture. Gilded woodwork on choir stalls, imposing altars, and the monumental organ provides an extravagantly decorative contrast to the logical, Renaissance forms of the structure. The carving, characterized by masses of intricate detail, is in a style called Churrigueresque. The term takes its name from the Spanish builder José de Churriguera, whose work in Spain, oddly enough, was far more restrained than the extravagant Mexican version of the style that bears his name. In the hands of local workmen, detail became more exaggerated and carved forms more energetic than in their Spanish models.

One of the finest examples of the Churrigueresque style is the Altar of Kings, which occupies the apse of the cathedral. In 1737, Geronimo Balbás traveled from Seville expressly to execute this altar as well as the high altar. He created an over-whelming maze of gilded woodwork, depicting a host of saints, cherubs, and angels.

The façade of the cathedral was also originally intended to be in the Churrigueresque style, but by the time it was built in 1786, Neoclassicism had become fashionable. José Damiano Ortiz de Castro, a native Mexican who was the architect at the time, chose a more controlled style for the exterior. He used Doric, Ionic, and the twisted Salomonic columns to arrange the façade into three-part divisions. The successful integration of his work, however, is offset by the squat towers which, by being too far apart from each other, give an unattractive, horizontal emphasis to the façade.

To derive some idea of the original intentions for the façade, one can look at the adjacent Sagrario Metropolitano, which was designed by the Mexican architect Lorenzo Rodríguez in 1749 and executed twenty years later at the height of the Churrigueresque style in Mexico. This charming building, an independent parish church that houses church treasures and the Holy Sacrament, provides one of the finest examples of the Churrigueresque still extant. The elaborate ornamentation is skillfully executed in high relief, with a multitude of saints carved amidst the luxuriant detail.

In spite of the riotous decoration, there is an emphatic vertical feeling in the small façade, which serves to relieve the richness of the embellishment. The enframing pilasters and flanking dark walls also provide a restraining contrast and serve as gradual transitions to the sober façade of the cathedral. Together, the two churches dominate the southern side of the Zócalo—the square that was already ancient when Cortes conquered Mexico nearly five hundred years ago.